The Multi-Age Classroom:

A Family of Learners

Wendy C. Kasten
Barbara K. Clarke

Richard C. Owen Publishers, Inc.
Katonah, New York

Library of Congress Cataloging-in-Publication Data

Kasten , Wendy C . , 1951–

   The multi-age classroom : a family of learners / by Wendy C .
Kasten and Barbara K. Clarke .
     p . cm .
   Includes bibliographical references (p .) and index .
   ISBN 1-878450-35-2
   1 . Nongraded schools . 2 . Education , Elementary — United States .
3 . Classroom management — United States .   I . Clarke , Barbara K . ,
1936–   . II . Title .
LB1029 . N6K37 1993
371 . 2 ' 54 — dc20   93-20195
                                             CIP

Front cover photography by Jack Elka Photography
Barbara Clarke's photo by Jack Elka Photography
Wendy Kasten's photo by Nancy Soles Photography

Richard C. Owen Publishers, Inc.
PO Box 585
Katonah, New York 10536

Printed in the United States of America

9 8 7 6 5

DEDICATION
TO JONI RAMER
AND HER FAMILY OF LEARNERS:
YOU WERE ALL OUR TEACHERS

PREFACE

In 1988, a teacher, Joni Ramer, came to us at the University of South Florida with an idea. She had just spent a month in New Zealand with Don Holdaway in classrooms that contained children from five to eleven years of age. Joni was very excited about what she had experienced, which was similar to the training she had received at Florida State University, and was more than a little anxious to become a teacher of a multi-age class.

We had just completed a study comparing whole language primary classes with traditional ones, and Joni's kindergarten had been one of the experimental sites in our study. Consequently, we knew the quality of her classroom and her teaching. It isn't every day that a research opportunity just falls into your lap like that, so we agreed to observe her multi-age class, just as soon as she could find a principal in her school district who would let her try out such a seemingly unusual idea.

To be honest, we were, in the beginning, only half-heartedly supporting her passion for multi-age grouping. Having had no previous experience with the idea, it was our faith in Joni's teaching that led us to pursue this. Because we were still writing reports from our previous study, we didn't have the time in the beginning to do any reading on the topic. We weren't seeking any grants for the study, and so we didn't even write the usual sort of proposal. We simply began visiting her new kindergarten class in August

1988, a class that would eventually grow into her multi-age, family-grouped class. And, as usual, we collected baseline data on these children in this low socioeconomic, ethnically diverse, neighborhood school, and we made periodic visits to collect naturalistic, narrative notes.

At the beginning of the 1989 school year, the school's principal added new kindergartners to the now first graders, thus creating a K/1 class. Again, we collected data and visited the class periodically. At the start of the 1990 school year, new students were added to create a K–1–2 class (class size remained the same, due to the fact that some children moved away). By now, we realized that this environment had something unique and special to offer that could not be duplicated in a traditional grade-level class—most especially that the original students had been with Joni for three years and there were about six sets of siblings in the class (a deliberate choice on Joni's part)! We originally intended to study the class for only three years, but when the fourth year came around, the school decided to keep the class intact and added a couple of new kindergartners. It seemed only logical that we would continue studying them.

This book is not about that study, per se, although our continuous learning about the multi-age context formed the basis of our knowledge to write this book. The specific results of the study will be the subject of another book in the not-too-distant future. This book evolved as a result of our speaking to groups on this growing trend. When our audiences, many of whom were parents and school board members as well as teachers and principals, asked, "What can we take home to read about this?" we discovered that the market was rather limited; and there certainly was nothing like this book available. That's when we decided we better buckle down, get to work, and write.

In this volume, we have tried to create something concise, reader friendly, and straightforward. With so many people asking questions, we hoped we could write a book that someone could take home, read in one evening, and come away with not only the information about multi-age grouping, but also the hopeful feeling that goes along with it.

The more we learned about multi-age grouping, the more excited we were. Actually, it goes further than that. The more we learned, the more we realized that grouping children like a family is a more logical and humane way to raise children, educationally speaking. There is no other place in life where kids are segregated, limited only to their agemates. We also realized that our Canadian, British, Australian, and New Zealand colleagues have known for a long time about the power of the multi-age classroom, and have a successful history with it. We have learned from all of them in various ways. And frankly, we are highly impressed with the effect the family-grouped classroom had upon our at-risk learners, our gifted learners, our bilingual students, our special education students, our late bloomers, and everyone in between. Does that sound too good to be true?

Think, for a minute. Isn't the family the oldest, most time tested, most successful model within the realm of human existence? Families are children's first and foremost learning arena, are they not? Not to mention the place we all received our emotional support, learned our social skills, our values, and our abilities to become loving human beings. Doesn't it make sense, then, to put these attributes into classrooms? We think it does.

W.C.K.
B.K.C.
1993

ACKNOWLEDGEMENTS

Seldom do researchers have an opportunity to spend four years in the lives of one teacher and the same classroom of children. We are greatly indebted to Joni Ramer, primary teacher "extraordinaire," and the children who lived and learned as a family at Samoset Elementary School from 1988–1992. They have contributed immeasurably to our knowledge of the best practices for educating young children, and provided us with a highly unique and valuable research opportunity.

Thank you from the bottom of our hearts, Joni and children, for enabling us to become intimate observers of your lives and classroom.

We would also like to acknowledge the assistance, time, and patience extended to us by Ms. Pat Heldreth, Coordinator of Primary Education for Manatee County, Florida; the principals of Samoset Elementary School during our study, Mr. Hillard Story and Mr. William Lance; and the wonderful and helpful staff at Samoset.

We are also indebted to some other teachers who shared with us their insight and expertise on this subject: Ms. Kathy Carmichael and Ms. Dale Woodruff, both of Leon County, Florida, and Ms. Johanna Scott and Mr. David Keystone, both of Victoria, Australia.

Finally, thanks to Dr. Eileen McErlain for her keen perceptions and helpful suggestions as she read this manuscript.

TABLE OF CONTENTS

CHAPTER 1
Understanding the Multi-Age Model

It is 1:30 PM on a September Wednesday in Ms. Ramer's class. The buses that take children home will begin arriving shortly after 2 o'clock. Until then, children have some free-choice time as the day draws to a close. Several children have gone to a chorus rehearsal for an upcoming event. Nickol and Oralia are sitting on the floor reading a book together. Nickol and Oralia, both African American children, are sisters; Nickol is a third grader and Oralia is a first grader.

Willy, an African American kindergarten student, asks Ms. Ramer, "Can I read?" He is asking to go to the classroom reading corner and choose a book he knows he can read. At the computer, first grader Natasha is teaching kindergartner Melissa how to use some educational software. Natasha is the youngest sibling of Nickol and Oralia.

Melissa's older sister, Ashley, is one of the three third graders at a table reading together a chapter of *Sarah, Plain and Tall* (MacLachlan, 1985). Both Melissa and Ashley are Caucasian children with long, straight blond hair.

Diana, a third grader, Elvis, a second grader, and Carla, a first grader, are at another table completing a math assignment, sometimes helping each other in Spanish. These three pupils are among the eight children in this class who speak Spanish as their first language. Diana and Carla are siblings. Elvis also has a brother in this class. Candy, still learning to speak English, skips across the room and asks a visiting adult if she can read a book to her. Candy's in this class for her second year.

All of this may seem unusual, but it is an ordinary afternoon in this multi-age primary classroom, where most of the third graders have been members since they were in kindergarten. Many of the second graders are starting their third year; first graders are on their second round; and only two students are completely new to the class. Among the current class count of 27, four grade levels, six age levels, and three ethnicities are represented. The total count will change in a few months when, for example, third grader Jesse arrives from Alabama as many migrant families return to Florida. Jesse will rejoin this class where he has been a member for three previous years, and will settle in to life as usual.

Whereas this classroom portrait may seem confusing or unconventional, it is actually the oldest working model of organization known to civilization: the family. This classroom depicts a family of children in an educational setting. The strengths of a family structure—which include such values as continuity, emotional support, respect, shared responsibilities, and cooperation—form the foundation of this classroom environment.

The idea of grouping children across grade levels or age levels is not a new one. In 19th- and early 20th-century rural America, the one-room schoolhouse, where children of various ages attended, was commonplace. Since then, however, the family concept has been introduced and implemented, and has been applauded as a positive innovation.

This book will serve as an introduction to educators, parents, and other interested community members who wish to explore the family grouping model, whether it be for curiosity or possible implementation. After four years of in-depth study of this model, we, the authors and researchers, find this model intriguing, promising, and potentially powerful as we look toward alternatives for restructuring the schools of the 21st century.

DEFINITION OF THE MULTI-AGE MODEL

Multi-age grouping, also referred to as vertical grouping or family grouping, can be any deliberate grouping of children that includes more than one traditional grade level in a single classroom community. The fact that such grouping is deliberate is important. Often a single classroom is created for economic reasons, as, for example, when a second and third grade class is combined because the school does not have sufficient children or teachers to create one class of each grade level. In this case, the teacher treats the group as two classes, each with different curricula.

Similarly, family grouping, vertical grouping, or multi-age grouping does not simply consist of multiple classes with multiple teachers where, for example, one or two of the classes are second grades and others are third grades; where children are taught different lessons by different teachers in a departmentalized fashion; and where the whole group sometimes gets together for an afternoon activity. Although these types of combined classes could easily become family-grouped, multi-age classes, they do not follow this model by virtue of their accidental grouping.

The family-grouped model explored here is a single learning community that becomes a cooperative, supportive, developmental unit. It is basically a single, normal-sized, self-contained classroom of children who represent two or more age or grade levels; it may include some siblings and/or cousins when available; and it is a heterogeneous group of children representing the intellectual, cultural, and economic profile of the school where the classroom exists. The grouping is not contrived to include, for example, only upper percentile second graders with lower percentile third graders. It is a random, balanced grouping from the school population, created with the support of the administration and participating teacher or teachers, the consent of the parents, and the best educational interests of the children in mind.

Another often referred to term within the multi-age literature is "continuous progress." Within our readings and our experiences, this term means many different things to many different people.

Some of the ways it has been used over the years differ drastically. For example, in the 1970s, continuous progress sometimes referred to the frequent evaluation and testing of children in order to monitor the incremental mastery of isolated skills. At other times, descriptions of "continuous progress" programs sound like they contain multi-age elements. Due to the ambiguity of the term, continuous progress will not appear within the discussions in this book.

Multi-age grouping is an organizational element of classrooms that we have observed as having the potential for both social and academic benefits. It is not, however, a panacea for an otherwise weak educational system if issues of effective teaching, strong and authentic curriculum, and positive educational leadership have not been addressed.

All the classrooms visited or studied for this book are the products of outstanding, whole language teachers, who opted to teach in some variation of a family grouping model. These teachers, all veterans of family grouping, feel strongly about the educational and social benefits of the model. As whole language teacher educators, we believe the element of choice is vital. Teachers who wish to try teaching a multi-age class may consider approaching their administration with a proposal. Administrators interested in implementing some multi-age classes might consider inservice programs or literature about the model (such as this book) to identify potentially interested and capable teachers (see Chap. 4).

HISTORY AND ROOTS OF MULTI-AGE GROUPING

Rural America has its own history of multi-age classrooms when scant populations dictated the one- or two-room schoolhouse. This was the only viable alternative to sending children away from their homes to receive a formal education. In the United States and Canada, only a few of these schools remain today, and they often have to fight politically for the right to remain in existence in the face of economic pressures and change.

The one-room schoolhouse offered certain attributes that were very sound educationally. First of all, children remained with the same teacher and primarily the same class of students for multiple years. School was a stable, reliable environment for the children who attended. Second, the mix of ages and abilities provided optimum opportunities for student collaboration. Older or more experienced students could assist younger or less experienced ones. Pupils were often needed to help each other and play teacher to other classmates, as there was only one adult with up to eight grade levels of children to teach. Older students served as role models for younger students, challenging them intellectually and socially. And there was no apparent ceiling on the content taught, discussed, or overheard within the room, which benefited older students by design and younger students more incidentally. Almost universally, adults who were products of one-room schools have fond, positive memories of their early schooling.

Capitalizing on some of these strengths, British educators planned and implemented a family grouping model to help heal the emotional scars of children who were sent away from their families during World War II. These educators viewed this model as potentially the most nurturing, supportive, educational environment they could create for a generation of children traumatized by the atrocities of war. In these primary schools, children were divided into three-year blocks of either ages 4–5–6, 5–6–7, or 6–7–8, and remained with the same teacher for several years (Connell, 1987).

Multi-age grouping is common in New Zealand, a country with the highest literacy rate in the world. In New Zealand children are permitted to enter school on their fifth birthday, and move along at their own pace that first year. These "early entrants," as they are called, are moved forward based on their achievement rather than on their chronological age. Differences among the children in abilities and interests are expected and celebrated as each child is socialized into the classroom community (Connell, 1987).

ASSUMPTIONS IN UNIT-LEVEL GROUPING VERSUS MULTI-AGE GROUPING

Every educational practice has some underlying reason that justifies its existence, whether it is verbalized; implied and unstated; based on sound educational theory and research; or simply invented from the traditions and bogus, prevalent thinking of an earlier era. According to Goodlad and Anderson (1987), the practice of unit-level grouping did not evolve from any research base. They traced this type of grouping to the Quincy School in Massachusetts, which opened in 1848 with a new plan for school organization that they predicted would set trends "for fifty years to come" (p. 44). Oddly enough, they under predicted the effect of their supposed innovation, which by 1860 had caught on, at least in more urban areas. Based on an industrialized model, the new system was believed to be economically sound, as it educated more children for less money, and was easy for administrators to monitor.

Alfred Ellison (1972) is another educator who discusses the anachronistic nature of gradedness as an organizational structure because of its disregard for individual considerations. The graded structure, Ellison argues, reinforces the use of graded series of textbooks, which has become a deeply ingrained educational practice. He points out that there is a "myth behind graded content" (1972, p. 212), and that graded classrooms and graded textbooks have little justification in research or in philosophy and, in fact, often become stumbling blocks to progress.

Our present system evolved and became a deeply ingrained tradition more by accident and economics, and multiple bogus assumptions are or became inherent in unit-level grading. These bogus assumptions can be contrasted with the parallel, research-based assumptions that underlie family-grouped models.

UNIT-LEVEL GRADING

Perhaps foremost among the justifications for unit-level grading, aside from the economic considerations upon which it was first based, is that **this type of grading presupposes a transmission model of teaching and learning**. In other words, it is presumed that teaching is mostly the oral delivery of knowledge and information, and that learning is the acceptance and absorption of this knowledge and information by students. The classic or traditional lecture-from-the-teacher format, which is teacher-centered, teacher- directed, and teacher-evaluated, is the format one expects to observe in classrooms. However, this once popular and accepted model is now considered delimiting as a method of teaching.

These next assumptions inherent in unit-level grading are closely tied to the more traditional transmission teaching model. For example, **unit-level grading assumes that children grouped within approximately one chronological year of each other will have similar learning needs and abilities, and thus will benefit similarly from instruction.** Because the teacher's organization of instruction will be tailored to the students' age, instruction will proceed logically, neatly, progressively; the children will earn logically, neatly, progressively. This type of grouping will minimize diversity, as diversity in this paradigm is viewed as problematic or less efficient for teaching.

This view of children can be compared to the industrialized model of assembly line production from which it came. Conjure up, if you will, an image of children as parts traveling along a factory assembly line. If all the parts are the same in dimension and quality, and the worker's job is to apply the same part or process to each item, then the resulting product will indeed be more complete and on its way to becoming a whole machine, car, or appliance. Standards for the finished product can fairly easily be set and evaluated with a reliable inspection. The problem is, of course, that in schooling we deal with human beings and not objects, and learning and development are not mechanized processes. Human beings, with their diverse background knowledge, experiences, and cultures, do not respond with the predictability of objects. Good teachers have always known this, even when politicians, tests, or materials tried to suggest otherwise.

This metaphor introduces another erroneous assumption underlying gradedness: **Learning is an orderly, sequential, hierarchical process.** Unfortunately, this view of learning has dominated educational thinking for many decades. This notion that learning is synonymous with training, or with stimulus–response behavior, causes educators to plan and implement strategies that treat human beings, especially children, with the same indignity with which researchers treated the animals used in the experiments upon which these beliefs were founded. It is somewhat incredible now to think that early behavioral learning studies (performed with animals responding to food rewards or electrical impulses) were ever generalized on faith to learning and development in human beings. Yet, for decades educators have lived with words like "mastery," "criterion referenced," and "behavioral objective," which equated learning and behavior as the same processes, and which were born of those early animal studies. More recent research regards learning as cognition, the process of knowing and perceiving, and identifies learning as complex, fluid, and dynamic rather than as hierarchical and sequential.

Again, in the mechanistic industrial paradigm, unit-level gradedness tends to assume that **there is only one teacher in the classroom, and that there are 20+ learners to be taught.** In this view, the teacher is thought of as having all the answers, and the children as having all the questions. It is assumed that the teacher's knowledge will be imparted to the learners, who will be complete, educated individuals when they, too, have all the answers. This would be sensible if knowledge were a finite entity, and we could equip children as a matter of course with every bit of knowledge and information that they could ever need in their adult lives. That is, of course, a ludicrous notion in a rapidly changing, technological world.

Today, as in the past, good educators try to promote the idea that the teacher is the number one learner in the classroom, and that education is at least to some extent the exploration of both teacher and student questions and answers in the community of the classroom.

The last assumption in the unit-level grouping paradigm is that **a year of schooling is not an educational process but a product with some standard upon which that product can be judged and rated,** similar to an article of clothing that any of us may purchase, which contains a tiny piece of paper in the pocket saying "inspected by number 13." This is the myth of a standardized grade level from which all children graduating have attained the exact same level of information and ability. Such a product-oriented view of learning and of curriculum has been promoted by series textbooks, by our system of standardized testing with resulting grade-level equivalences assigned to achievement, and by annual, sequential promotion to the next grade level.

Often, in order to help parent or teacher groups understand this point, we ask them to consider their knowledge of children learning to walk, for example. Young children learn to walk at a variety of ages, anywhere from 8 to 15 or 16 months. The period between 12 and 13 months is often cited as an average. The differential between these periods for walking is really quite vast when you consider that a few months is a large percentage of a young child's lifetime. Yet, parents expect children to walk at different times. And children who walk prior to their first birthday are not generally thought of as accelerated walkers, advanced walkers, or gifted walkers. Nor are children who walk after their first birthday admitted to remedial walking classes or thought of as retarded or delayed walkers. By the time they enter kindergarten, there are no clues as to which children were the early or late walkers, and there is no correlation between the onset of walking and children's ability or intelligence. So why should teachers and parents expect certain predictable outcomes from a year of schooling, when we know that this assumption defies everything we know about child and human development?

MULTI-AGE GROUPING

Probably the most important, inherent assumption upon which multi-age grouping is based is **the view of a teaching model that**

is interactive in nature. As is fundamental to most whole language settings, the classroom does not operate primarily on a transmission teaching model. That is to say that, although there are times when the teacher may directly teach a lesson to the entire class, it is also likely that during the day a variety of learning and teaching contexts will be observed. Examples of varied contexts may involved students clustered into "centers" to work in pairs or in small groups, without a teacher immediately present; teachers meeting with individuals or small groups; and children sometimes engaged in independent study.

While many of these different learning–teaching contexts can be observed in many unit-level whole language classrooms, the difference in the multi-age setting might be that the groups contain children of different grade levels much of the time, resulting in older children modeling for, helping, or even teaching other students. This cross-age collaboration is productive for both the helping student and the student being helped. The children being helped have a kid role model and receive kid-to-kid explanations, which is very different from adult teaching. They get multiple teachers, and a clear vision of where they are headed academically. The helping children are stretched as they must bring their knowledge to a conscious level, choose language for explanation, and develop an increasing sense of responsibility and self-esteem. Helping children are constantly reminded of what they know, and develop attitudes of themselves as capable individuals.

In the multi-age classroom, **student diversity is a given**. While astute teachers have always recognized the breadth of diversity in any class, in this setting diversity is considered a classroom strength and is central to making the learning community effective. Some writers have suggested that positive effects of diversity can be illustrated by considering, for example, a parent with several children.

Imagine the different issues that arise for a parent of three children if (a) the three children are each two years apart in age; or (b) all three are exactly the same age (as in triplets). Parents of multiple birth families have talked about the stress of having more than one child who needs mostly the same kinds of attention at the same time, as opposed to having multiple children whose needs vary. In the latter scenario, parents and children can work together in many ways to meet everyone's needs. In the former, a great deal more burden rests solely with the parents.

A multi-age classroom can operate more like a family operates to solve its everyday needs. Different people have different jobs, and increasing responsibility comes with advancing age and experience. Older siblings at times have to help out younger siblings, but this does not in any way detract from the quality of the older child's growth and development; in fact, it may even result in earlier maturity.

In the multi-age classroom, the teacher capitalizes on the diversity of age and experience to strengthen the environment both academically and socially. Getting to know the ways children differ in skills, experiences, and natural talents can benefit the learning community. Children can contribute in a variety of ways, ranging from who's a good speller to who can debug the computer; from who's good at changing the paper towels to who can mix paints well or reach the highest shelf. While any good classroom capitalizes on learner strengths, in the multi-age classroom, teachers can more readily utilize the varied and more diverse strengths and abilities available to them.

Another basic underlying assumption within multi-age groupings is **a different view of the learning process.** Contrary to earlier concepts of learning as sequential, hierarchical, and fitting into neat and orderly patterns, a dynamic view of learning is accepted within the multi-age whole language classroom.

To understand this difference, let us consider our own ways of learning. Most adults who understand their own personal learning realize that they typically do not learn about something new in a neat and orderly manner. Any adult who acquired her first computer within the last decade should have evidence of this. Look at it this way: How many readers can honestly say they read their computer manual before touching the keyboard? The typical new computer owner learns to use the computer by playing with it, asking questions, trying out different functions, and making mistakes along the way. Most adults consult the manual intermittently, or when mistakes occur. Those fortunate enough to have a disk giving an introduction to the computer might ask themselves exactly to what extent it was helpful. Did they remember everything it taught them when they needed it later? Did they ever forget how to do something after someone had told them about it, or after they had learned about it?

Most people (or kids) forget some things, especially those things they did not have a chance to practice or use in any real, functional way. They learned or found out about the things they needed first, and their skills grew as they became good at the basics and gradually widened the scope of their experience with the machine. They learned by doing.

Multi-age groupings are based on the notion that learning is dynamic, complex, and saltatory. That is, it has progressions and regressions along the road to growth. Learning is developmental in the sense that learners can proceed to tackle more difficult things as they acquire knowledge and understanding. But learning is not, and never has been, tidy or orderly; and we'll all be better off when we stop trying to make it, package it, and assess it as though it were.

Another assumption that underlies the multi-age concept is **a view of curriculum.** Because unit-level grading made certain assumptions about the sequential nature of curriculum, it operated with myths about standards set for accomplishment. Multi-age grouping views curriculum more from a process approach, acknowledging the value of learning **how to learn** as much as **what to learn.**

Because the acquisition of knowledge is infinite, one of the most fundamental features of multi-age grouping is that it does not presume that education can "cover" everything. For in a sequential, hierarchical view of curriculum, "cover" becomes an overused word that to some extent denotes the depth and quality with which a subject or topic has been treated. When quality is sacrificed for quantity, the outcomes are not desirable. Under those circumstances, units of study are neither memorable nor thought provoking. In a race to "cover" more material, facts, or information, there is little, if any, attention given to more substantive, critical thinking, or "higher-order" thinking skills as they are sometimes termed. Such skills involve analysis, comparison, evaluation, synthesis, and other processes that require more than merely scratching the surface of facts; they are essential in enabling learners to be in charge of their own, continuous, lifelong learning, and for participation, perpetuation, and promotion of a democratic way of life.

Finally, within the multi-age classroom model, it is assumed that **the teacher will facilitate a variety of teaching and learning experiences that will be developmentally appropriate for students in the class, and that children will learn what they can from those experiences.** In other words, there are times when agemates work and learn together, and other times when non-agemates work and learn together. Each person participates to the fullest extent of his or her current abilities and experiences. What each learner always sees is the context in which his or her task or part makes sense, as well as a vision of what he or she will be learning to do in the near future.

For example, in one multi-age primary, children are grouped differently throughout the day. In the morning, the teacher has children working at "centers." At the listening center, where children listen to audio tapes of quality children's literature, she will have at least one child present who is somewhat older and more proficient at operating the tape recorder. This will help the center run smoothly, as well as ensure the longevity of the tape recorder. At a writing center, where children are progressing on various types of writing assignments, having children of mixed abilities provides role models, helps answer most student questions, and facilitates rich interaction.

Conversely, there are other times during the day in this same multi-age primary when students are grouped more with their agemates for other kinds of instruction. For example, the kindergarten students within our research class are grouped from time to time for specific work on counting, letters, or colors; these are skills the other children have long since mastered, and the teacher may decide some direct instruction with the youngest children is indicated. Later the same afternoon, the most experienced readers meet together to read *Sarah, Plain and Tall* (MacLachlan, 1985), which is still too difficult for many others in the class. Sometimes, with their teacher present, and at other times independently, this group reads the book aloud together, writes about their reactions to the book, and chooses different literature extending activities to complete cooperatively.

SUMMARY

Multi-age grouping, or vertical grouping, in which children of more than one grade level or age level are deliberately grouped to form a single learning community, is a logical and time-tested manner of educating children. Building on the strengths of family structures, and the strength by which those structures have proved successful for thousands of years, family grouping in schools also has a logical and promising foundation.

The last century has been the only time throughout the history of education when children were consistently grouped and administered in structures that separated and segregated them according to a calendar criteria. Segregating agemates, a practice based on an industrialized model, was not implemented as an innovation that would be good for children, and has no basis in theory or pedagogy. In fact, segregating children by ages assumes a teacher-centered classroom style, assumes children of same ages are the same in development and needs, and fosters unrealistic expectations for outcomes.

When children are grouped diversely by differing ages, there are inherent assumptions that are more consistent with our knowledge about what is good for educating children, and the nature of child development. This practice, common in rural America and in other countries, provides an optimum environment for reasons that promote both the social and academic well being of children. These benefits are discussed in depth in the next chapter.

CHAPTER 2
The Benefits of Multi-Age Grouping

Educators, parents, and school board members who are potentially interested in family grouping for their schools will want to know how this model will benefit their children. Their first concern is learning. Will our children learn more? Will they learn better? In this chapter, we will address the two major benefits—academic and social— and we will examine these from the viewpoints of other writers and researchers, as well as from our own observations.

WHAT OTHER WRITERS AND RESEARCHERS HAVE TO SAY ABOUT ACADEMICS

Many of the sources that address multi-age, family-grouped models are either unpublished research reports or articles that are more than 20 years old. Only a few recent sources are available. Nonetheless, their collective reports show a recognizable pattern.

These various reports share the results of studies in which direct comparisons were done between some type of multi-age model and a traditional unit-aged model (children of the same age). All of the studies use published standardized measures such as achievement tests containing various subtests in verbal and/or mathematical areas.

Before considering these results, it should be noted that standardized tests are a quantitative rather than a qualitative assessment. That is not to say that they are not valuable, only that the value should be tempered with the tests' inherent limitations. Because educators now better understand the limitations of testing, tests of these sorts are no longer considered the educational gospel of assessment they once were. First of all, tests assess only two areas of intelligence, math and language. Second, they are written with content more familiar to mainstream children than minorities, thus producing cultural biases. Third, tests employ a format of multiple-choice questions which represents narrow, convergent thinking rather than broader, divergent, higher-order thinking. And finally, the rigid formality in which tests are given can be an intimidating experience for learners, and may produce a single result that is not representative of the learner's typical or best work.

In view of, or in spite of, these limitations, studies show that children in multi-age or family-grouped models score either similarly or better academically than their comparison peers in traditionally grouped classes. For example, some reports showed that multi-age grouped children scored more favorably, at least at some age levels, than did other children (Carbone, 1961; Hamilton and Rehwoldt, 1957; Buffie, 1963; Gilbert, 1962, 1964; Morris et al., 1971; Schrankler, 1976; Connell, 1987; Gajadharsingh, 1991). Within some of the reports, children in the family-grouped models scored better in certain verbal skills, whether these skills were reading, vocabulary, or other language-related skills (Halliwell, 1963; Hillson et al., 1965; Milburn, 1981; Connell, 1987).

Of the areas we might consider language skills, vocabulary development is most often cited as at a considerable advantage for children participating with mixed-age peers because they receive maximum verbal stimulation (Day and Hunt, 1975; Graziano et al., 1976; Lougee et al., 1977; Way, 1979). Sometimes within the same study multi-age classes scored either better or the same as their comparison peers, depending on which measure was used (Schrankler, 1976). Other studies showed multi-age grouped children scoring better in mathematical reasoning, whereas other subtest scores such as reading or language were comparable to those of their peers (Steere, 1972).

The fact that academic achievement is often a payoff in multi-aged groups may be explained in the work of Piaget and others (Piaget, 1947; Pontecorvo and Zucchermaglio, 1990), who describe how mixed-aged interactions stimulate disequilibrium, equilibrium, and cognitive growth, especially in the less mature individuals participating in the interaction. In other words, younger children may persist for less time in erroneous thinking, mis-generalizations, or other developing but inaccurate hypotheses about the world because of the presence of the older or more experienced children. The social support of the group stimulates an environment where disagreement, argumentation, and resistance are all conducive to thinking. These dynamic processes support and encourage children's growth much as "the air does the flying bird" (Pontecorvo and Zucchermaglio, 1990, p. 69).

There are some writers and researchers whose work or beliefs suggest that academic achievement between multi-age groupings and unit-aged groupings are not appreciably different, and that the value in family grouping is in the social realm, not primarily in the academic one (Ford, 1977; Pratt, 1986). Only one study claimed that students in the unit-aged classes achieved more than multi-age grouped children (Carbone, 1961).

In summary, most studies found that multi-age grouped students performed better academically, both in reading and in math; some found them doing approximately the same; and only one found students not doing as well academically. All these results should be read cautiously in view of the fact that very few of these studies addressed the quality of the curriculum or the teaching process, and only one of them (Pontecorvo and Zucchermaglio, 1990) used any qualitative assessment, such as an example of children's written composition.

One could interpret the summary of these results in a number of ways. Perhaps the important aspect of multi-age or family grouping is not an academic one, but a social one. Or, possibly, the classrooms used may have varied greatly in quality, climate, and ambience. If, for example, many of the classrooms used were poor or mediocre classrooms and the only difference was the grouping, then it may be remarkable and noteworthy that many of the multi-aged groups scored better academically, and the presence of mixed peers did somehow influence their learning and achievement.

Although on the surface the reports of all these studies appear inconclusive regarding the academic value of innovative grouping, we believe there is enough evidence to constitute serious food for thought about the impact family-grouped classrooms can possibly have on learning and on achievement. There is a need for careful classroom research utilizing qualitative measures to document the impact of multi-age groupings.

WHAT WE HAVE OBSERVED ABOUT ACADEMICS

After four years of visiting and studying multi-age classes, we do have a sense of the optimum learning opportunities that occur by the day, hour, and even minute that would be less likely to occur in a traditionally grouped class. Often, children cannot learn in either a large or a small group, and there is no alternative except individualized attention to help them through something difficult. Yet, how often can a teacher devote even half an hour to a child who may desperately need special attention?

In the multi-age class, we have observed moments, whether they were planned and manipulated by the teacher or happened spontaneously, when one child has taken the time to teach another child the very thing he or she has been struggling with. While peer teaching and tutoring can take place in any classroom, when the teaching child is one or more years and grade levels ahead of the child being taught, the potential benefit is considerable. The benefits of such an arrangement to younger children are obvious; but older children benefit as well. In helping a younger child, the older child must bring his or her knowledge to a most conscious level and synthesize it in order to teach it. Pairing an older child who is not an expert on the given topic is prudent, because the older child is forced to raise his or her level of understanding, and thus confidence is strengthened.

Another phenomenon that occurs quite naturally within multi-age settings is the powerful influence of role models. Role models allow developing children, who are absorbed in their own work or their own learning, to have a vision of where their knowledge or skills are headed. It is almost as if the child in the unit-graded class wears, to some extent, a visor to shield the view of what is above or ahead, like the horses that once pulled milk carts or ice wagons. Whereas the horse could look solely ahead, the child's peripheral view looks to the sides, down, and around, but never up. In the multi-age grouped class, the entire panoramic view is available, and the class ceiling of learning possibilities is higher.

Recently, we had occasion to spend time with Jonathan, a first grader, who is particularly gifted. This is his first year in a multi-age class after attending a kindergarten which was traditional, structured, and where no authentic, connected writing experiences took place. In his present class, he was invited to write in a journal the very first day of school. Jonathan informed his teacher that he could not write. When she insisted that he could write, and insisted that he try his best, he began writing letter-like forms and some known safe words like "love."

One-half of a school year later, Jonathan wrote lengthy stories that filled two or three pages in his journal in small, single-spaced manuscript. This rapid and unusual growth happened because Jonathan's models of writing were not the other first graders, but second or third graders. Developmentally, he was more similar to the older students in his ability to communicate in writing. In a regular first grade, where Jonathan would have been the top student, he would not have had another student to look up to. But because he did, he advanced to his best potential and not that of his agemates.

Another point for consideration is that in the multi-age class, the vocabulary and content are geared toward the upper end of the class. Though teacher expectations of performance are always geared toward each child's individual abilities, children are exposed to more sophisticated oral language and more sophisticated content topics. Again, one might say it's as if the ceiling has been lifted.

In order to understand this point more thoroughly, consider once again the dynamics of a family working together. Imagine, for example, a family on a camping trip. Let's say there are four children, ages five, six, seven, and eight, with two adults. Thus, the content topic is "camping knowledge," which might include outdoor cooking and housekeeping, tent setup, fire building, camping safety, and living close to nature.

If various tasks are assigned to each child based on the adults' views of appropriateness and ability, then the chores might end up something like this: The eight-year-old helps one of the adults put up the tent and load the sleeping bags, gear, and air mattresses into the tent to prepare for bedtime. The five-year-old is assigned to assist the other adult in the preparation of food, which will include setting the picnic table for dinner. The six- and seven-year-olds are paired and instructed to fill water containers needed at the campsite and collect kindling wood for the fireplace. Let's assume that everyone does his or her assigned task at least acceptably, though minor mishaps would be natural and expected.

At the end of the day, can it be said that the eight-year-old is the only child who knows anything about putting up a tent? Has the five-year-old's learning been confined to the realm of the picnic table?

No. In such an authentic learning environment, all the children now have an overall notion about what camping entails. Even if only one child helped to erect the tent, all the children have learned that a tent is erected with stakes and poles, with some way of fastening the tent to those poles and stakes. And they have a vague concept of the time it takes to put up a tent. The five-year-old learned quite incidentally what kindling wood means, and everybody knows at least something about each other's jobs. If we had taken a group of five-year-olds and put them in a different location and taught them to collect kindling, then the only content they would have learned that day would have been about kindling. We could, of course, continue to build on this knowledge, bit by bit, working our way up to an eventual camping adventure. However, the first scenario portrays a much more practical, authentic, and efficient learning and living opportunity.

In our family camping unit, the five-year-old knows that at some time in the future he will learn to put up a tent and, most likely, looks forward to it, as it is associated with more grown-up knowledge. None of the children feel either inferior or superior to the others, because they realize that with increased age comes the ability to learn different and more difficult things. There is no stigma attached to anyone's current level of camping knowledge (achievement).

If you can see the intricate implications of four children all participating in a camping experience, then you can begin to see the power that role models have in an environment for introducing children to other aspects of content and for keeping in perspective the larger picture of the whole.

The longer we study the multi-age model, the more we come to understand the powerful influence of role models. From an academic standpoint, this is a climate that cannot be duplicated in a classroom where children are grouped by the same age or grade level. In fact, trying to account for differing abilities in a unit-graded classroom is difficult because the opportunity for comparing and mentally rank ordering children exists, whether or not the idea is acknowledged or sanctioned.

A student who needs to request help may be hesitant to ask an age-mate for fear of seeming inferior. But requesting help from an older child is a normal, expected behavior among children, with no stigma attached. In classrooms where such collaboration is so frequent, it eventually becomes completely natural to ask any classmate for help, regardless of their age.

MULTI-AGE GROUPING AND SOCIAL ISSUES

It's just possible that the most important part of this book, and of this entire issue of grouping, is what you are about to read here. That is not to say that the other areas are unimportant, nor that the issues of academic and social benefits are entirely separate; they are actually quite interrelated. But the more we explore the grouping issue, the more we realize that from social or logical standpoints the system we have created and made our tradition is neither natural nor logical when educating human beings.

WHAT THE LITERATURE SAYS ABOUT SOCIAL ISSUES

Whereas the literature on academic values for multi-age grouping had some inconsistencies, the authors and researchers who have written about its social benefits have been universally full of praise. Various writers have outlined the value of multi-age groupings for increased pupil self-esteem, increased general student maturity, increasingly positive attitudes about school, and even better relationships and attitudes in dealing with parents.

For example, several studies looked at students' attitudes toward their education and their schools after one or more years of being in a multigraded classroom. Each of these studies showed students having more positive attitudes toward school than students in more traditional classes (Schrankler, 1976; Milburn, 1981).

Other studies looked at various aspects of self-esteem and maturity in children who attended school in multi-age classes (Buffie, 1963; Stanton, 1973; Hammack, 1974; Schrankler, 1976; Connell, 1987). Each author has a great deal to say about the social value of multi-age grouping, noting an observable or documented advantage for children within mixed-age settings as to better or more positive self-esteem. Other writers summarize what they believe are both social and academic benefits arising from multi-age grouping: The creation of more independent, intellectually mature learners (Wolfson, 1967; Ridgway and Lawton 1965; Moorhouse, 1970; Muir, 1970).

Other researchers look at social aspects of mixed-age grouping in a different way. Some studies have demonstrated that children in mixed-age grouping tend to show more nurturing and support to classmates than do children in unit-aged groups who reportedly show increased aggression and competition toward each other (Wakefield, 1979; Hartup, 1977, 1979). Interestingly, the increase in aggression and competition when similar agemates are grouped for extended periods of time has also been observed in animal studies of other primates (Pratt, 1986)! Higher-order primates and human hunting/gathering societies that have survived into the 20th century also socialize and educate their children in mixed-age play groups (Pratt, 1986). In other words, grouping children in mixed-age settings is natural; grouping them in same-age settings is not.

Another study supporting the idea that children in multi-age classes show more nurturing, altruistic behavior within the classroom and toward classmates was done by Bizman et al., (1978). Still another study simply describes young children in these types of settings as more sociable (Goldman, 1981). These are important goals to consider when preparing students of today for the social and academic challenges of the 21st century.

BIRTH ORDER EFFECT IN THE CLASSROOM

One pair of writers thought extensively about the relationship between children's birth order and their intellectual development, and how these interact within a conventional classroom (Zajonc and Markus, 1975). Another writer, Virginia Stehney (1970) raised a similar point about children's position in the classroom when she observed that multi-age grouping enables both teachers and students to look at each learner as an individual, and that each child's relative social position within the room never remains the same for very long. She observed that, as a result, pupils were better able to make personal and social adjustments.

In other words, consider those children you have known, who by the luck of the draw were very youngest, least mature, least developed children in a typical unit-graded classroom. If these children progressed adequately, then they were promoted every year of their academic life, but probably always remained at the lowest end of the classroom profile both intellectually and socially.

After five or six years of this pattern, how do these children view themselves as learners? Do they see themselves as capable and competent, and do they harbor high aspirations? How likely are children at the low end of the spectrum to envision themselves as future doctors, lawyers, teachers, leaders, or in some other job that may require confidence? Yet, children's relative position may not reflect their potential, and in a multi-age setting, no child remains in the same position among the classroom profile for more than a year.

What We Have Observed Concerning Social Issues

It is difficult even to know where to begin this topic, because the material and feedback we have collected on multi-age classrooms is truly overwhelming. Perhaps our observations can best be summarized by sharing a real story about a particular child.

When the classroom we were studying became a combined kindergarten, first-, and second-grade class during the 1990–91 school year (it had been a K/1 the previous year, and five new kindergarten students were added to the veteran class), there was one child named Willy, who was young not only because he was one of only five kindergarten students, but also because he barely met the age requirement for school entrance. And, on top of that, he was a late bloomer.

When we first met Willy, on his second day of school, we had very strong reservations concerning his placement in kindergarten at all. He had virtually no social skills. He had never, to the best of our knowledge, touched a book. He had no notion about even the existence of letters or words, not even those in his name. In addition, he was an extremely active child, with a tendency to get into mischief.

Many teachers have had a "Willy" in their classes, and typically the prognosis for school success for such children is not good. Willy was a potential discipline problem as well as one who would require much personal attention. He would most likely be difficult to educate; in the beginning, Willy misbehaved quite often and had frequent visits to the principal's office.

One year later, Willy had been through kindergarten and was in his second year in this multi-age classroom. He still knew very little about letters and words, although he did by then love books, and could read a few simple ones. The remarkable thing was that at that point Willy acted like a responsible student, and no longer stood out from the rest of his class. He attended to stories and tasks, appropriately, and fit into the general social organization of the group.

Willy's teacher felt that the change was not because of anything she did, but rather was due to the group dynamics. At some point, the other children no longer condoned his extremely childish behavior, and Willy somehow responded. Based on our combined experience, we feel strongly that in a group of his age peers, Willy would be a continual headache for both his teacher and his class. The environment of his agemates may even have fueled his immaturity and perhaps encouraged the immaturity of other classmates.

In Willy's case, it would seem as though the presence of role models and peer pressure by older students had an incredible impact on his socialization. Frankly, we continue to be amazed by his progress. It is this aspect of multi-age grouping that may be the most compelling as we consider alternatives for the students of today.

CHAPTER 3

The Classroom as a Community

As we visit outstanding classrooms and outstanding teachers, one common denominator we find memorable is the teacher's ability to create a sense of community in these classrooms. A desirable attribute in any classroom, a sense of community, may be easier to create in the multi-age setting because of the diversity of strengths found among the class members. Just as in any community, different people have different jobs, and each is to some extent interdependent because of developed specialties and interests. Thus, diversity becomes the community strength.

In a multi-age class, diversity similarly becomes a strength. Utilizing the experience, capabilities, and interests of different children makes community participants depend on each other for making that community work. Because of these varied abilities, interdependence can be fostered rather than having all of the responsibility rest solely upon the teacher. Again, this is similar to a family structure where different family members clean the house, prepare meals, supervise the laundry, or contribute to the family income. The difference between the family and the multi-age setting is that the multi-age setting has a trained professional at the helm who can facilitate learning, capitalizing on each learner's strengths so that responsibilities are shared, changed, and benefit the most children possible.

This chapter shares some vignettes collected from real class-rooms. Hopefully, this narrative camera will show what the multi-age classroom might look like to an observer. In these anecdotes, either one or both of us are present.

AN INTERMEDIATE MULTI-AGE CLASSROOM

This anecdote comes from a rural suburban school. The children are mostly Caucasian or African American. The school is located in a middle-class neighborhood. Kasten is the observer present.

It is 2:00 PM and Mrs. Smith's multi-age fourth and fifth grade is having their "center time" for the fourth time during the school day. Centers are cooperative groups that are either self-selected or teacher assigned, where students work without direct teacher supervision. The assignments or directions for centers are posted within the room in particular locations, usually on a clipboard or a nearby chalkboard.

At one center, the children are together reading a play from a book. A student at this center acts as group leader to help assign parts and regulate the work. In another part of the room, children are working on math assignments that are individualized and in file folders with their individual children's names on them. A science center is also in use and students at this center are assigned a topic to study in a science book, which they will later be required to teach to the rest of the class.

At one table in the room, Mrs. Smith is teaching a lesson to approximately six students. She is addressing a particular skill about "quadrants" in math, and relating it to using latitude and longitude on a map or chart. Still another center is completing a specific assignment on decimals.

As these centers progress, noise levels in the room are regulated carefully by the use of overhead lights. When lights are turned off, children know that they have become too noisy and they are automatically reminded to lower their voices. This is obviously a well-practiced management strategy, because no words were spoken, only the dimming of the lights and the quieting of the groups were evident.

As this room hums with its business and engagement, there is absolutely no way for an observer to tell who are the fifth graders and who are the fourth graders. On the wall, the daily schedule is posted:

8:25	Eye Opener
8:40	Guidance/music, physical education, etc.
9:30	Total group— teacher
10:15	Center I
11:00	Center II
11:55	Lunch
12:25	Silent reading or Center II continued
12:45	Center II
1:30	Read aloud and developmental play
2:00	Center IV
2:45	Dismissals begin

Although the teacher of this multi-age class would describe her class as fairly "immature," she also reports that no one is ever bored in the class, and there have been no incidents of unacceptable behavior all year. Because of vast differences in abilities, Mrs. Smith reports that she begins the year reading much of the material, both pleasure reading and informational, to the class. No one reads aloud until they volunteer, she states firmly. It is because of the consistent modeling, she believes, that one particular child who was still nearly a non-reader at the beginning of the school year now reads fluently and volunteers readily to read aloud in class. She also reports that because of the nature of these particular students and their age groups, she spent the first five weeks of the school year working on and studying about self-esteem.

At 2:00 PM, presentations begin by one group of students whose job it was to study the respiratory system of the human body, plan how to teach their information to the rest of the class, and be prepared to present their lesson orally. One child from the group goes to the front of the room where the overhead projector and screen are set up. He has drawn a diagram of part of the respiratory system and explains the inhaling and exhaling process of breathing and the organs involved.

As the teaching child proceeds, the class and the teacher are all taking notes. The teacher asks questions to help clarify or summarize certain points, treating the child as the expert on the subject. A second member of the same group gets up next; his job is to teach specifically about lungs. He has prepared an overhead and uses a pointer as he is delivering his prepared talk. The audience of his peers asks some questions to clarify his points, and he answers many of them very confidently and knowledgeably. The classroom teacher shared later that this presenter is a fourth grader and, according to school records, considered to be "severely learning disabled."

Another student gets up to make a presentation on the trachea. He has also prepared a diagram on a transparency, talking for about two minutes on his topic. Some classmates ask about the epiglottis at the top of the trachea, and he responds well, explaining its nature and function. The next members of the respiratory group, two girls, get up to present their portion of the lesson on the diaphragm. They have prepared a poster that they hold up containing a diagram to which they refer in the presentation of their material. They have pre-written their explanation, which they then read aloud while the class takes notes.

Next, the same two girls hand out a crossword puzzle that the group has prepared, which reviews information about the respiratory system and which is a follow-up assignment for each class member as homework. When students complete the assignment, it will be handed in, evaluated, and returned to class members by the group who was responsible for today's lesson. As this lesson is completed, it is close to dismissal time and students prepare to go home.

A KINDERGARTEN/GRADE ONE MULTI-AGE CLASS

This anecdote comes from a working-class, lower socioeconomic neighborhood where few parents have completed high school. The class has a multi-cultural profile including Caucasian, African American, and Hispanic children. Some of the latter are from migrant agricultural families who move twice each year to locations where pickers for fruits, vegetables, or cotton are needed. Both authors are present.

It is 8:41 AM, and the children in this class are still trickling in as buses arrive, which are slightly behind schedule. Most children spend this free time looking at or reading books in the book corner. Nicole, a first grader, has stopped by and asks to read one of us a story. She assumes we'll agree, and so she begins reading even before either of us has a chance to say yes. Nicole's reading is an approximation of a familiar story, which is both predictable and easy to read. In other words, she is "reading" using similar language to that of the actual print which is an important early reading behavior.

The teacher calls the class together on the floor in the area where all group lessons are conducted. Because both of us are in the room today, the teacher reintroduces us as Dr. Kasten and Dr. Clarke, taking the opportunity to review how both <c> and <k> can make the same sound. Ms. Ramer asks the children what day it is, and someone says it is Thursday. She asks them what is special about the word Thursday, and someone says that it begins with /th/. The teacher reminds them that /th/ is called a digraph and asks for other words that begin the same. Someone says "thought" and she praises that child's response.

A girl from another room comes in and shows a snake and some bird eggs that she has found. The children enjoy looking at the specimens. Ms. Ramer asks the class if anyone knows how to tell the age of a snake, and no one seems to know. So she further asks "How could we find out?" One child says you could find out by going to a snake shop. The teacher asks for more ideas, and someone says "at the zoo" and another child says "museum." Still another child says that a museum is for dinosaurs. Abel, a first grader, tells about some items he saw at a flea market made from snake skins. Nick, a kindergarten student, says he saw stuff at a flea market that looked like snakes but they were really made of glass. The teacher tries to redirect the conversation and talks about how scientists preserve things in formaldehyde, and also asks what it is called when a snake loses its skin. She gives a hint that the word she's looking for also begins with a digraph. She further hints that cats and dogs do it in summer, and that it can also be the name of a building in a back yard. Someone finally says "shed."

Nick volunteers that he once saw a poisonous lizard shedding its skin and it was "gross." Michael, a first grader, says he also saw a snake once. The class discusses skin and shedding a while longer.

At 9:08, Ms. Ramer begins a "shared reading experience," which consists of words to a song on large paper, poised on the easel so everyone can see it. Children follow the words chorally, just as they would for a story. Different children take turns using the pointer to follow the text for the benefit of the class as songs proceed. Thus, this time, which appears more like a music lesson or just an enjoyable time together, is actually a reading lesson. They sing several songs including "The World Is a Rainbow." Ms. Ramer takes this moment to reiterate how the song teaches us that people are different and unique, but that it takes all kinds of people to make the world.

At 9:14, Ms. Ramer and her class move on to more shared reading. This time, children are asked to choose which of the many class-generated lists or stories posted around the front of the room will become reading practice for today. The class by consensus chooses one butcher paper mural covered with words and phrases about Christmas. They discuss the word "Christmas" and how it does not sound like other words that begin with <ch>.

One child suggests that they talk about the /sh/ in the word sharing, and so they volunteer other words that begin with /sh/ as do some other items in their room. The teacher asks who can come up and read all the words. A first grader, Brittany, gets up and reads flawlessly all words and phrases on the chart. Nicole, a less mature first grader, gets up to try. She reads the ones she knows and says which ones she does not know, and so everyone reads those words together. She is praised for being able to read so many.

Nick, a kindergarten student gets up next. He can read the title and a few other words. Everyone applauds. Abel, a first grader, volunteers next. He needs quite a bit of help finding a few words he can read, but the positive response from the teacher is the same. Krissy volunteers next. She is a kindergarten student, and can read just a few words or phrases. The teacher reminds her that it's okay to read only the ones you know and skip the others. Krissy does this and receives praise.

This continues a little longer, and then the teacher gives directions for the center time coming up. At the writing center students will be working on Christmas stories. At the math center everyone will be making a counting book. The counting book will consist of individual pages where the child will write the numeral one and paste one item on that page, and continue in the same manner up to the number ten for kindergartners and up to twenty for first graders. Everyone knows they can play "number bingo" when their work at the center is completed.

A few students will be at the reading corner during this center time, and two children will be permitted to paint at the easel as their center. Everyone will be busy at these centers for about an hour.

As the centers proceed, there will be both kindergarten and first-grade students at each center. At the writing center, all children will be working on a new page in their Christmas book, which consists of five or six pieces of drawing paper and a sheet of discarded wallpaper stapled together. Their assignment each time they attend the writing center, approximately every second school day, is to draw something related to Christmas and to write something that goes with the picture. This book will take two to three weeks to complete.

Children will begin working on their new page first by drawing. Different children will be developmentally very different in regard to their understanding of writing. Ms. Ramer will spend part of this center time seated with this group. She will discuss writing with the youngest children, modeling how they should think about what they wish to write, listen for the sounds they hear in those words, and to try their best to write what they believe they heard.

A few children at the writing center will be inexperienced and will have little idea of how to proceed. For those children, Ms. Ramer will suggest that they dictate to her what they wish to say and she will write it for them, modeling the correspondence between sounds and words. Some children will produce writing that bears little resemblance to conventional writing. Because these are early approximations, they will be accepted, and the children will be asked what they wanted the writing to say. The intended message will be added by the teacher, perhaps at the bottom of the paper.

A few children at the center, some of the grade one students, will proceed with little need for direction. Although their writing may not be spelled conventionally, it will likely be readable with the support of the context of their pictures. These children writing at the center also serve as role models for the less experienced children who see what is meant by the teacher's directions. Children will readily help each other, reminding each other how to form a particular letter, or how to write a particular word. This group support is part of the community that serves to promote educational growth through the natural assistance of classmates.

A K–1–2–3 MULTI-AGE PRIMARY CLASSROOM

This anecdote comes from the same classroom as the previous one, only two years later. The children mentioned earlier, such as Sheila and Nicole, are now third graders. Nick is a second grader. Some students have changed as children moved away and class members were added. Kasten is the observer.

It is 1:30 PM on a Tuesday, and there is approximately one hour of the school day remaining. Sheila, a third-grade student, is sitting just inside the door reading an anthology of horse stories. Robert, another third grader, is reading *Sign of the Beaver* by Elizabeth George Speare (1983) in another part of the room. Ashley and

Brittany, both third graders, are reading a novel together at a table. Willy, an immature kindergarten student, and Elvis, a first grader, are on the floor doing an activity that requires them to identify letters of the alphabet. Dante, a third grader, is at the computer table also reading a novel. Carla and John, both first graders, and Nick, now a second grader, are playing with some blocks. Several members of the class are out of the room attending speech therapy, a special class for second language learners of English, or receiving services of the special education teacher. This time of day is used for catch-up, completion of various assignments and, in some cases, a free choice of educational activities.

Natasha, a grade one student, stops by to share her writing which she has spent 30 minutes working on. There are real letters arranged into groups that look like words but aren't. There is no evidence yet of any letter/sound correspondence in her writing. Becoming literate is moving slowly for Natasha, as it did for her sisters Nikkol (third grader) and Oralia (second grader). Nikkol now reads fluently and enthusiastically, and Oralia is a beginning reader. Natasha's pretense of orally reading her story results in a two-minute elaborate storytelling about a trip to an Italian restaurant.

Luis, a second-grade bilingual student, shares the journal entry he has just completed about a field trip to a local historical site. Candy, a kindergarten bilingual student whose English is still blossoming, is playing a board game with Melissa, a third grader. Candy soon tires of the game, and brings a book that she asks to read to me. Her reading is a close approximation of the story and text.

Michael, a third grader, his brother Johnny, a first grader, and Jesse, a third-grade migrant student, are reading educational magazines from the classroom reading corner. Oralia is also in the reading corner, nested in a bean-bag chair reading a book by Maurice Sendak.

A few minutes later, Michael, Jesse, and Willy go to the listening center and select a tape and corresponding book by author/illustrator Arnold Lobel. The teacher, Ms. Ramer, is at a table working with kindergartner Elvis and first graders Nick and Ruben identifying letters of the alphabet. All three of these children are still very much emergent readers. She then reads a predictable story with them, taking turns with children reading to the group, pointing out features of print.

Marvin, a third grader, is working alone, recopying a letter to his pen pal. Marvin has great difficulty with spelling, and so Ms. Ramer had provided him with a list, correctly spelled, of words he misspelled in his letter. He has the task of matching the conventionally spelled words to his invented ones prior to recopying.

Melissa, a kindergarten student, is playing with math manipulatives on the floor. Melissa is a younger sister to Ashley, a third grader. Robert, a third grader, is playing a number game with Justin, a first grader. Everyone remains engaged in some appropriate, selected activity until ten minutes before the bell, which will call children to board the first school bus. Now, clean-up and dismissal rituals interrupt individual activities.

A GRADE 5/6 MULTI-AGE CLASS

This anecdote comes from a working-class suburban school outside a major metropolitan city, where many parents of the children are unemployed because of the closing of a local plant. The children in the class are primarily Caucasian and Turkish immigrant children.

This class has recently visited a local park to learn about ponds and estuaries. The teacher reads to them in a reading corner where students are gathered on the floor at her feet. The selection is an informational book about ponds and streams. She asks them to recall things they saw on their recent trip and then she resumes reading aloud.

Students are then provided with a sheet of paper with ten animals drawn on it that live in a pond or estuary. She directs them to color in the fauna according to the real colors these life forms might have, using resources in the room as needed. After completing the coloring they are further directed to select either a tan or blue piece of construction paper for background, onto which is drawn the shape of a pond. Then they are to place the cut-out animals from their sheets either in or around the pond as their habitat requires, and draw in the appropriate flora. Their finished product will have a sheet of cellophane added over the top of the construction paper to give it an aquatic look.

As students proceed with their projects, they occasionally get up to observe the aquarium that has recently been constructed within the classroom, and the species they have collected. This helps them decide on the colors of crayon or marker to use in shading the animals or the plants. The teacher discusses with the class how, at the end of their study about ponds, the creatures will be returned to the pond where they were collected. As they continue to work, they are occasionally reminded to stay on task.

This classroom is arranged with tables and chairs, and plastic bins hold students' personal belongings. An ample classroom library has multiple copies of both novels and nonfiction books available for group literature study. There are also single copies of favorite novels, some picture books, and informational books on a revolving book rack like many found in bookstores. Hanging from the ceiling are mobiles that illustrate the food cycle in pond habitats, as well as other student-produced work.

As in other anecdotes, there is no way an observer can distinguish the fifth graders from the sixth graders. The class is functioning effectively as a community.

SUMMARY OF VIGNETTES

It may be a surprise to the reader that these classrooms look very similar to classrooms where students are age segregated. While their organization may differ somewhat from a unit-aged classroom, it does not change as much as one might expect. The issues of organization are dealt with in Chapter 4. As a matter of interest, one of the vignettes included here was collected in Australia. The others are all American.

CHAPTER 4
Implementing Multi-Age Models

This chapter will offer advice. The suggestions are the opinions of the authors, which were formed as a result of extensive research, and after consultation with teachers and principals experienced with multi-age grouping. Hopefully, readers will find these guidelines useful as they review current multi-age classes, or perhaps plan and implement the first multi-age classes within a school or district.

As in other parts of this book, we are presuming that classrooms in question are already effective, whole language environments, full of both joy and rigor, with interesting, meaningful content. A change in grouping should not be considered a "fix" for a classroom, teacher, school, or curriculum that is lifeless, ineffective, textbook dependent, boring, or somehow inhumane. Those kinds of difficult issues require a commitment to staff development and other educational reforms that this book does not offer. These are merely guidelines for reviewing or implementing multi-age grouping; we assume that outstanding teachers will be involved.

The rest of this chapter will be divided into two major sections with multiple subtopics: The first section is a guide for administrators who seek to implement or expand multi-age grouping in a district or individual school. The second section is for teachers, and focuses on the transition to multi-age models in terms of individual classroom planning.

IMPLEMENTING THE MULTI-AGE MODEL: NOTES FOR ADMINISTRATORS

As we stated before, this section presupposes that the teaching and curriculum in the school are current, theoretically sound, and holistic. These guidelines are for principals, superintendents, or other school district personnel who wish to move toward multi-age models beginning with an administrative initiative.

SELECTING TEACHERS FOR THE MULTI-AGE MODEL

As firm believers in teacher choice, we believe that any school or district contemplating new multi-age classrooms should involve teachers in the decision process. Providing prospective teachers with visitations, inservice, or current reading material (such as this book) may assist in a self-selection process. In other words, teachers who might wish to become involved in a new or changing multi-age setting should have the opportunity to elect to participate. Where this is not possible, teachers should still be consulted, valued, and invited into the process of change. Change is never as smooth or effective when it is mandated or imposed. Teachers bear the burden of all classroom changes; their participation should be paramount in the change process.

For teachers unfamiliar with multi-age grouping, school administrators can help make arrangements and provide release time for teachers to visit conveniently located multi-age classes. Spending a day or two with a veteran multi-age teacher and students will likely be more persuasive and informative than any other inservice strategy. Also, this generally can be accomplished with minimal expense to the school or district.

We once had the opportunity to host a delegation from a neighboring district who were interested in exploring multi-age grouping. This district sent several prospective multi-age teachers, a principal, one school board member, and a parent representative to the classroom where we were conducting our research. After one day in the classroom, these educators, who had driven three hours to visit our site, left not only enthusiastic, but impatient to begin plans for their own multi-age classes. A school visit can answer many questions and concerns easily.

Another consideration for selecting teachers for multi-age models is peer support. In any change, it is important to consider having someone with whom one can talk, plan, troubleshoot, and interact professionally. For example, if an administrator is considering starting two multi-age classes—one in the primary grades and one in the upper grades—then neither teacher would have adequate collegiality. This would make change more difficult and less effective. Starting two (or more) primary mixed-age classes and two (or more) intermediate-grade classes would provide for peer support among the faculty, and a smoother transition.

Another factor to consider when selecting teachers for new multi-age classes is the level of respect from parents those teachers have earned. One principal reported that because the teachers she chose were so highly regarded by the school's parents, the parents' sense of confidence and credibility in the idea was increased.

PARENT COMMUNICATION

Every administrator knows that parent involvement and support can make or break any idea or program. Consequently, educating and advising parents of upcoming plans is extremely important prior to implementing change. In many areas, there will be few, if any, parents who have ever heard of a multi-age classroom, let alone have any experience with it. Therefore, the school has the responsibility of educating them about the concept.

Existing parent–teacher organizations can be vital in this process. Inviting speakers, sponsoring panel discussions, and perhaps showing prepared videos can all be helpful. Many parents will want to read further on the topic. The school can create a succinct handout with key information, provide copies of articles on this topic, or even lend copies of this or other books.

In the many parent forums we have conducted, we have found it helpful to compare this model to the way a family functions; this is something parents are knowledgeable about. Explore with them the manner in which multiple children are raised at home. Many parents will come to understand the logic quickly, and it is likely that they will raise the same questions posed in Chapter 5.

Continued parent communication should be maintained throughout the school year, highlighting events from multi-age classrooms. Many schools use their school newspaper or newsletter for this purpose. The biggest selling point for the program will be the children. Parents want their children happy and well educated. When they see that these goals are being met, they will support the multi-age model.

SELECTION OF STUDENTS AND THEIR GROUPINGS

On a fundamental level, we believe that a multi-age environment is better for children than a grade-segregated one. It is a more natural way to educate young human beings than the system many of us have lived with in the latter part of the 20th century. Nonetheless, for a school beginning multi-age classes for the first time or reviewing existing multi-age models, there are a few guidelines we can offer.

First of all, we feel that however the selection of students proceeds for the multi-age classes, those classes should be similar to other classes in the school in size and in academic and social profiles. We have discovered that a common misconception circulating among parents and teachers is that multi-age classes contain either all gifted children or all lower achieving students. Neither is true, nor appropriate. Educators have long known that grouping children with others of very similar abilities is counterproductive, at best, to most students, and can have dire consequences.

Multi-age classes should be heterogeneously arranged. In other words, the composition of the class should consist of children with diverse abilities and interests, no matter to which potential grade designation those children belong. There is no type of child for whom this setting would be educationally inappropriate. There are others for whom this setting might be optimum.

When educators are considering placements for a new school year, then one particular type of child does come to mind when multi-age classes are an option. This is the child whose development begs for the support of a family-like setting, whether it be for the need of older role models, a need for a sense of continuity or responsibility, or just a supportive daily environment.

Such a child may be one whose life has gone through enormous changes, or who needs an environment to develop new kinds of social skills. As mentioned in Chapter 2, this family-like environment is associated with bringing out nurturing, altruistic behavior, and minimizing aggressive and competitive behaviors. Of course, loading any classroom with too many needy or at-risk children will not constitute a workable learning community. A balanced classroom profile—children differing academically, socially, and ethnically—is the most logical and sensible approach.

In both Australia and New Zealand, where multi-age models are commonplace, groupings of either two grades, three grades, or the entire age 5–11 spectrum are found. Some educators feel that any of these groupings are workable, but that grouping four grades together may result in children having a more difficult time finding something in common with each other.

For teachers trying a multi-age class for the first time, a grouping of two grade levels may be an easier transition than taking on three grade levels. From some of our local schools that are beginning to implement multi-age models, we have learned that it is extremely helpful to create the first multi-age classes with a core of students from the teacher's class the previous year. In other words, take a second-grade teacher, let 8–12 of her second graders remain in the class as third graders, and add new second graders to form a composite two–three. We have also discovered that it is somewhat easier for many teachers to go up in grade level (such as a second grade teacher moving into a two/three) rather than going down in grade level (as in a third grade teacher moving into a two/three).

Teachers need time to adjust their expectations, and it seems to be somewhat easier to look forward.

Another popular and highly promising variation was suggested by a veteran multi-age teacher from Victoria, Australia, David Keystone. This model involves about 50–55 students with two teachers in a single learning community. For this type of grouping to work, regardless of the multi-age levels selected, it is imperative that the two teachers work well together. Keystone points out that having one male and one female teacher is an added plus, as it gives children the opportunity to see men and women working together in constructive, positive ways. The presence of two positive role models better serves children of both genders.

Whether the two teaming teachers are one gender or not, the opportunities for collegiality are powerful. Having two heads for planning, two minds for brainstorming about problems and needs of particular children, and two points of view on every learner is beneficial. In addition, Keystone and his former co-teacher, Johanna Scott, remark on the benefit to teachers of having a reliable colleague for emotional support as part of a team. If one teacher is not feeling so well, the other can carry the extra load for the day. If one teacher is frustrated or impatient with a child, the other can provide balance and perspective. In this case, both teachers and their 50 plus fifth and sixth graders function as a single classroom in a double-sized room, planning the entire week together, sometimes taking turns with the planning of a sequence of lessons or a special event. The result was a highly successful classroom.

INSERVICE AND CONTINUED SUPPORT

The first inservice that might be offered for a school contemplating change should probably be offered to the entire staff with some parent representatives. Perhaps a veteran teacher of multi-age grouping might provide a workshop, which could outline for everyone the nature and workings of multi-age grouping.

Follow-up inservice in the way of discussions, brainstorming, and planning with potential multi-age teachers might logically follow. Allowing ample time for teachers to talk out their planning and curriculum concerns with each other will help them feel more excited and committed to the idea. These types of discussion and planning times might need to take place periodically throughout the first several years of multi-age operation. In these sessions, teachers can talk about parts of their day that work well, raise questions about parts of their classrooms that do not work effectively, and negotiate solutions to each other's concerns.

Another level of inservice, occurring perhaps once or twice during the year, should involve parents. These inservices might be, as mentioned earlier, accomplished through the parent/school organization with programs open to the public. In addition, principals in schools with multi-age classes, either new or veteran, might plan one or two get-togethers both with themselves and their concerned teachers to discuss issues that arise and to lend support.

SCHOOL SUPPORT STAFF AND SPECIAL AREA TEACHERS

When changes in school occur, in any way, shape, or form, all school personnel are affected. Special teachers of music, art, physical education, special education, and other areas of specialty need to be included as well in the inservices. These teachers, like their peers, have also become accustomed to teaching children of unit-aged classes. They may have organized their curriculum around developmental experiences and be uncertain as to how to adapt to change.

Principals can remind these special area teachers that outside of schools, children's activities are not set up in age-segregated fashion, but rather by groupings similar to multi-age classes. Girl Scouts and Guides, Boy Scouts and Guides, and children who belong to community sporting events are also grouped with several age ranges. Similarly, children who attend group dancing lessons, martial arts instruction, or other after-school activities are not segregated by grade level.

As special area teachers rethink the presentation of their curriculum, they can look to these models to gain insight into the dynamics of teaching across age levels. Many of these teachers have probably at times held jobs when they did in fact teach children of multiple ages, whether it was at a camp, community center, or other facility.

In some cases, it may be appropriate for special area teachers to coordinate their participation with classroom content. If adequate communication and flexibility exists, art teachers may be able to focus on art that is related to the science or social studies of the classroom. Music teachers might do likewise by coordinating music programs to enhance content area study. The potential of these specialists to communicate the cultural aspects of different countries, ethnic groups, and time periods is indeed a gift to the classroom teacher. We visited a music classroom where that teacher's focus on African instruments, music styles, and dance was coordinated with several classrooms who were studying the African continent and highlighting the rich heritage of the African American students in the school.

PROBLEMS AND ISSUES

To date, there have been few if any problems we have observed that would be of concern for administrators. The only real issue has been change, which can be difficult to accept. In other words, the age-segregated system is so entrenched in so many areas, that the idea of changing it seems ludicrous to some parents and to some teachers as well. They come with their genuine concerns, but often a very narrow paradigm of what schooling should look like.

This issue is not different from those any school might experience with any other change. Schools that gradually changed to holistic teaching methods most likely had a similar experience with educating parents gradually, with some people accepting the new ideas more readily than others. Remembering that parents react out of true concern for their children is important.

Administrators should be well informed and able to document from professional books and journals the changes in their school or district. Helping parents and other community leaders understand that changes locally are part of the larger realm of educational changes throughout their country can be helpful and lend perspective. Just as physicians have the burden of educating their patients as to new procedures and methods in medicine, schools have the same role in keeping the public informed about its changes. Both disciplines are essential to people's well-being.

IMPLEMENTING THE MULTI-AGE MODEL: NOTES FOR TEACHERS

This topic is actually too vast for a mere book section but, nonetheless, a few words of advice might be welcome. We would advise teachers to read Chapter 5 carefully, as it addresses questions both you and the parents of your children may have. The best advice on implementing a multi-age class will come from other teachers and from your own storehouse of ideas as well.

Many strategies and systems that are used in a unit-aged class are either the same or similar to those in a multi-age class. Not everything done in the past needs to be thrown away or changed. If you already offer a variety of developmentally appropriate experiences for your students, then you already have a sense of planning for and meeting the needs of learners.

CHILDREN OF DIFFERENT LEVELS

First of all, like any class you have previously taught, a multi-age class is just a class. They are 20 plus children with varied backgrounds and needs that you will begin to discover with your new school year. They are a single class, and a single learning community. You may be surprised to find that their characteristics do not seem particularly different from those you encountered in an age-segregated class.

Veteran multi-age teachers will usually say that you "teach to the top of your class" in terms of vocabulary and directions but with appropriate expectations depending on individual abilities. Novice multi-age teachers have shared with us that at the beginning of the school year they could not teach to "the top of their class," but as the year progressed, they became more comfortable with this.

We know from child development studies that children do not develop in even or predictable patterns. Nor is their development steadily paced as they proceed. Learning, as well, is not neatly sequential or tidy, although in the past we have taught as though it were or ought to be. No doubt you observe this in your daily teaching. View your pupils for their individual characteristics, strengths, and weaknesses regardless of their age or grade designation.

Feel free to vary the way you group students at different times. As noted in the vignettes in Chapter 3, there are times for whole-group instruction in many whole language and many whole language multi-age classrooms. There are also times when children are grouped by interests, by needs for special attention or special challenges, and by who will work well together. There are also times for children to work independently.

Times of the day when all students and the teacher are engaged in personal silent reading (such as "Sustained Silent Reading" or "Drop Everything And Read") are not different in multi-age classrooms. Similarly, in a process approach to writing when children are working on their own stories, a multi-age environment does not differ except in the range of capability that will be present. Content areas may require a different manner of planning, at least somewhat.

CURRICULUM PLANNING

In classes where teaching is done primarily by theme, teachers report that they plan a two- or three-year sequence of topics in science and social studies. These two areas are not entirely separate; for example, a science theme, like "the sea," can pertain to topics in social studies as well (communities that depend on the sea, economic implications of water pollution, political issues with offshore oil drilling, etc.). In communities where certain topics are traditionally required at particular grade levels, teachers plan to teach them within the long-term sequence. For example, if a fourth grade is required to learn state or provincial history, and a fifth grade is required to learn national history, then the teacher of the four/five multi-age teaches one topic the first year and the other the second. Certainly there is nothing sacred about when topics are taught and learned.

In other districts, teachers have more latitude to choose topics of content study. Therefore, they may make their choices based on student interest, community appropriateness (i.e., children in coastal communities may need more content about coastal issues), or political changes in the world (topics about the Middle East or Russia are more popular than they were 20 years ago).

For some new multi-age teachers, mathematics teaching was the biggest adjustment in the multi-age setting, because they were accustomed to either a graded textbook or a particular set of objectives. As in reading, children vary greatly in their development and learning of quantitative concepts. Teaching some subjects to the entire class (such as graphing, measurement) may be appropriate. Yet other topics might be handled individually or in "centers" (such as practice at computation, experiences with manipulatives). The best part of the multi-age model is that the teacher has more "teachers" in the class. The teacher can explore ways to use the knowledge of your more experienced mathematics students to encourage or model math concepts for the less advanced students. This may take some trial and error and/or discussion with other multi-age teachers to generate ideas for teaching particular concepts or issues.

In any event, it is important to remember that we cannot teach our students everything; the realm of knowledge is far too infinite. We can teach them to love learning, and the skills to become lifelong learners. For example, nearly every teacher today is computer literate to some extent. Yet, nothing in most of our education could have prepared us for this eventuality. We cannot predict the world which our children will inherit any more than our own teachers could have done so many years ago. The foundations of critical thinking, problem solving, and an attitude about lifelong learning are far more important than any particular content.

CLASSROOM ORGANIZATION AND MANAGEMENT

The descriptions of classrooms in Chapter 3 may offer concrete suggestions for classroom organization and management. There probably are many parts of the classroom organization that do not need change. Any aspect of classroom organization that can be accomplished by the children instead of the teacher should be. Each task contains potential learning value, even things as simple as cleaning up, preparing centers, assembling bulletin boards and displays, mixing paints, or changing the roll of paper towels at the sink. Pairing older and younger students for certain tasks to promote apprenticing situations is something to be considered.

Many multi-age teachers use a "rule of thumb" when grouping for centers or other cooperative activities to make certain that there are both more experienced and less experienced children in nearly every kind of group (unless they have been grouped for specific instruction because of an identified need). This way, a more experienced child answers questions for the less experienced, solves many problems of the group, and avoids unnecessary interruptions. Good structuring of groups in this manner releases the teacher for instruction with small groups where intervention is the most purposeful use of teacher time.

PARENT COMMUNICATION

Perhaps utilizing parent volunteers in your classroom is already in place. If it is, this parent participation can serve as wonderful public relations to other parents and the community. If parent volunteering is indeed an option, this kind of assistance can be very helpful.

When contemplating parent involvement in your class for the first time, it would be wise to take the time, perhaps in an after-school or early morning session, to train your volunteers in the manner you wish to best utilize their help. For example, modeling for parents how to respond to student writing, how to read to young children, and how to listen to emergent readers can be supportive to your program. Often, we make assumptions about what parents know. Taking the time to educate them somewhat can go a long way in supporting our educational outcomes.

Many teachers already have in place effective parent communication channels, such as a newsletter, phone conversations, or parent–teacher conferences. These effective avenues should, of course, be continued. Again, it would be relevant to ask yourself if there is any way some of your capable children can assist in the communication process. Perhaps a student-produced newsletter on the class or school computer might take the place of a teacher-produced one. Such a newsletter can become part of the language arts program, providing authentic writing experiences for class members.

One other avenue of communication might be to frequently invite parents to student events. Periodic class plays, the reading of student-produced books, or the dramatization of a story in children's literature might be good times to extend invitations. Even if only a few parents can attend, the experience is valuable for both the children and the parents.

PROBLEMS AND ISSUES

To date, all the issues that newer multi-age teachers have reported to us have to do with their own adjustments to the different ways of teaching. Typically, teachers report that it takes several months, and occasionally longer, for them to feel confident about themselves in their setting. No teacher has shared with us any concerns that result specifically from the class being multi-aged. Sometimes teachers share concerns about a less cohesive class of students. However, this is due to the combination of personalities rather than the multi-age grouping, and can happen under any circumstances.

Several teachers have expressed the feeling that it was more difficult to adjust their teaching of math than any other aspect of the curriculum. Other teachers report no difficulties at all with change. "They're just a class," one teacher said, "and I don't think it's any different from any regular class I've taught." Only one teacher we've met expressed a desire to return to a unit-aged classroom. Another said she felt equally comfortable in either and it made no difference to her. Still others are adamant that they hope never to have to teach an age-segregated class again. They feel strongly that they deal less with discipline issues and consequently have more time for teaching.

One of the most difficult problems that new multi-age teachers have had to face is having to defend the new program to an occasional confrontational parent before that teacher has had time to become comfortable and confident with the new paradigm. Typically, these are parents who did not participate in available inservice and informational programs. In these situations, we feel that teachers need administrative support. Early on, questions may best be filtered through the principal or another administrator who has the needed supportive documentation to share with the concerned parent.

All new endeavors take time. Becoming accustomed to a new way of teaching or organizing will not happen immediately for most teachers. Patience along with support will be helpful.

CHAPTER 5
Questions Teachers and Parents Most Frequently Ask

As we participate in conference presentations, parent–teacher meetings, or informal discussions with teachers or parents on the subject of multi-age grouping, much of our time is spent answering questions. To many, grouping children of differing ages into one class is a new concept; to others, the concept may not be new, but it is baffling. Unit grading is ingrained in the fabric of our schooling. Considering the organization of classrooms in which three, four, or even more different ages of children would reside requires a shift in our paradigm of schooling and in how we think learning occurs.

In this chapter we would like to address six of the most frequently asked questions pertaining to multi-age grouping. We interviewed two teachers in Tallahassee, Florida, Dale Woodruff and Kathy Carmichael, who have years of experience with multi-age primary/elementary classrooms. One of us spent a sabbatical teaching at a university in Australia, where she interviewed two veteran multi-age classroom teachers, Johanna Scott and David Keystone. And, certainly, we have relied heavily on the generous sharing of philosophy, beliefs, practices, and life of Joni Ramer in whose multi-age classroom we have spent much of the last four years. The answers to these six questions are a blend of their collective knowledge.

QUESTION 1: HOW DO YOU DEAL WITH STUDENTS ON SO MANY DIFFERENT LEVELS, REQUIRING SO MANY DIFFERENT CONTENT AREAS?

The underlying assumptions in this question are somewhat faulty. Do all children of the same age have the same abilities? Do they have the same background experiences? Do they all have the same breadth and depth of knowledge on a particular subject? Do they all have the same interests, motivations, tolerances, learning styles, aspirations, etc.? We think not. No fifth-grade teacher has a group of children who are all exactly alike; he has a group of individuals who just happen to be about the same age, and age may be where their similarities stop. Some teachers who have taught both types of classes, multi-age and unit graded, report that they have had unit-graded classes with wider ability ranges than their multi-age classes.

Good teaching requires that we consider each student as an individual. Multi-age grouping may even make it easier to see our children as individuals because we are forced to assume difference rather than likeness.

As teachers plan instruction for multi-age classes, the issue of what content to teach naturally arises (such as in science or social studies). One teacher reported that when she taught a group of five- to seven-year-olds, she simply concentrated the first year on the content required by the district for kindergarten; the second year, the content required for first grade; and the third year, the content required for second grade. The following year she started the cycle over again. All children, therefore, were exposed to all required content, and there was no overlap. Another teacher selected content required for all levels of children within her class, combined and selected broad areas, and taught similar content each year, going into more depth and breadth each succeeding year.

Using an integrated curriculum, and trying to involve all different subject areas and the content from those areas into one topic, seems actually to lessen the effort the teacher has to make to reach all the different content areas. Keep in mind that content subjects are simply the modes or means of teaching the processes the students need. After all, all children in one grade level do not come with the same experiences and are, therefore, not going to leave any content with the same information. This is similar with any collection of children, regardless of the grouping pattern.

We have referred to multi-age grouping as family grouping; and, as in any family setting, the teaching is typically directed at the highest level of learner in the group. One would use vocabulary and language patterns appropriate for the highest level, but stop and clarify points as needed. This clarification step is not always employed, however. Sometimes the younger children just get out of the experience what they can. This exposes the younger children to a much richer world than they would otherwise have.

An example of this can be pulled from the family archives of one of the authors, who has four children. When the youngest, David, was born, the oldest, Cathy, was two and one-half years old, and the twins Cindy and Bobby were in the middle. (Ignore the warning that is flashing in front of your mind: "Why am I even considering the opinions of someone who had four children under three years of age!") When it was time to toilet train the middle twins, Cathy was already a fairly adept "potty" user. Bobby and Cindy, therefore, had the model of someone who was pretty much their size, still thrilling at the joys of accomplishment, and anxious to be the teacher in their new venture. Bobby and Cindy, despite the fact that they were chronologically the exact same age, did not progress at the same rate nor have the same degree of success. Cindy would have this great spurt of success, while Bobby would be in a slump. Bobby would make a great leap forward, and Cindy would seem to forget that she had ever seen a toilet.

Cathy, all the while, was gaining confidence and self-esteem in her role as "leader of the pack," whether she was acting as model, coach, or encourager for the twins, or simply keeping little David entertained on the sidelines. David, in the meantime, was at times observing and interested, at other times oblivious to the hoopla going on around him. When it eventually came time for David to approach this important phase in his development, he already had a fairly good grasp of the vocabulary, the concept of what was going on, what his responsibilities were, and what was supposed to happen. It was a much easier process for David. In fact, there was little conscious effort required of anyone to teach David this critical life skill.

It is the same in any classroom, regardless of ages/abilities included in the group. It is much more effective and expedient to have a family of learners among whom there are many teachers and many learners, than to have one teacher and all the rest learners.

QUESTION 2: IN A MULTI-AGE CLASSROOM MODEL WON'T THERE BE GAPS IN THE CURRICULUM AND IN THE CHILDREN'S LEARNING?

No two children come to your classroom with exactly the same needs. Whether moving from state to state, school to school within the same district, or just moving from one teacher to another in the same school, there is no guarantee of one continuous curriculum. The theory of "covering the curriculum" is ludicrous, anyway! We cannot begin to teach students everything we believe today they need to know; even if we could, our views of what they need to know would change by next week. And who makes the decisions about what these critical pieces of information are? Topics are politically or socially more correct at some times than at others. Once the pendulum has swung back, and the previously inappropriate information has gained credibility, what do those of us do who did not learn it in school?

It is obvious, then, that content is simply the means we use to teach students what they need to know, **how to learn**. Looking at the metaphor of "covering the curriculum," we can readily see that it is a misnomer; something that covers is thin and unsubstantial. If we try to cover too much, there is really no mastery of anything. We need a more substantial amount of information in some areas so we can get into higher-level or critical thinking skills. With depth there is a high level of engagement, the kind of engagement that makes us lifelong learners. It gives us a sense of pride and confidence to know a lot about a topic. It gives us even more security to know that, if there is any subject about which we choose to know more, we are capable of easily acquiring that knowledge.

Our final comment on this question is that we all have gaps in our knowledge, regardless of how intensely a teacher tried to affect the scope and sequence of our learning. The reasons for this are myriad. We may have been absent from school some days; our teachers may have been absent from school some days; the ideas we were taught were later refuted; or the knowledge had not been discovered or invented yet. Each child comes to the classroom as an individual. It's not important that we try to teach kids everything. What is important, is that everything that's taught is taught well.

QUESTION 3: AREN'T THE OLDEST OR BRIGHTEST CHILDREN BORED OR HELD BACK?

Think back to the story of the Clarke children. When Cathy, the oldest, needed to learn how to use the toilet, she was not held back. Nor was there any special problem of working this into the routine of the rest of the family. In addition to being able to wear "big girl pants," Cathy derived other benefits. She was regarded with admiration and respect by her teachers (parents) and her students (the younger Clarkes). She parlayed this early leadership ability and success and other experiences like it into a lifetime of being an eager and accomplished learner and leader.

In a multi-age classroom, the child's position is constantly changing. One year she may be among the younger children, knowing less but eager to learn from and fit in with the older ones. The next year, new children may enter who are younger than she. She will continue to look to the older children for knowledge, but she will take on the added responsibility of being a guide for the younger ones. Eventually, she will be among the oldest in the group, knowing some things just by virtue of having been there the longest. Research in the effects of birth order on the academic and social achievement of children confirms that the oldest child is typically a higher achiever, with more self-confidence and social skills (Zajonc and Markus, 1975).

Our observations, and those of multi-age teachers with whom we have talked, support the idea that this phenomenon also occurs for the oldest children among multi-age groups. A perfect example of a "brighter" child not being bored is Sheila, who is among the oldest and brightest children in our multi-age research classroom. One day she wrote to an adult pen pal that third grade was "getting harder and harder every day." She obviously was not bored and did not view the class as too easy for her. She was always being challenged. On one visit to the classroom, we observed Sheila reading in an anthology of horse stories. She was engrossed in a popular horse story, and stated that she planned to read all the stories. The reason Sheila and the other children in Joni Ramer's classroom were not bored is good teaching. Good teachers find ways to challenge the brightest students, including letting them explore their own interests. Sheila had such an opportunity one year with architecture, when a new wing was being added on the school. Because of Sheila's interest in architecture, arrangements were made for her to meet and interact with the school architects.

Ironically, when our study was completed and Sheila was promoted, she was placed in an ordinary unit-aged grade four class. In her new setting, Sheila was intolerably bored as everyone was expected to do similar work. As a result of parent/teacher and parent/principal conferences, Sheila was immediately promoted to grade five to relieve her boredom.

Sometimes older children play teacher. Teaching something to another person forces the teacher to bring to the conscious level all that she knows about something, and to become thoughtful about what she does not know or clearly understand about the topic. Good and challenging teaching is the secret to keeping all children meaningfully engaged, regardless of group or placement within the group.

QUESTION 4: DON'T THE YOUNGEST CHILDREN IN A MULTI-AGE CLASSROOM FEEL OVERWHELMED OR INFERIOR?

No, the youngest children do not feel overwhelmed or inferior! Both the social and academic learning which are required of the youngest children in a multi-age group seem to come much more naturally and fluidly when they have the models of children of differing ages, abilities, and accomplishments from whom they can learn. It is easier, as we have said, for a child to feel secure and comfortable in a family of learners who provide support and nurturing, but whom he can also observe struggling to learn new things. Think back to the example we used in Chapter 2 of the family camping trip: The youngest had an important contribution to make to the camp-out, yet was not expected to do things beyond her abilities. All the children were comfortable with their jobs/contributions, everyone benefited and enjoyed the experience, and no one felt his or her job was more important than anyone else's. The family was working and learning together, both socially and academically.

One of us interviewed several university students in Australia who, as children, had been both in unit-age and multi-age classrooms. They responded heartily that they loved being the youngest, as they learned so much from the older children and felt almost privileged to be with them at school.

In classrooms that have different levels of children working in holistic, cooperative fashion, this same family atmosphere exists. We have observed kindergarten children entering Joni Ramer's multi-age classroom and have been astounded at how quickly they are socialized into the classroom. They have older children modeling appropriate behavior, guiding them in knowing how to line up, how to clean up after an activity, how to participate in shared reading activities, how to sit and listen to a story, how to paint at the easel, etc. By the end of the first day, it is virtually impossible to tell, except perhaps for the differences in size, the new kindergarten students from the class veterans. In many unit-aged kindergartens, the children are somewhat overwhelmed the first day of school because they are surrounded by children just as uncertain and inexperienced as they are. Only the teacher knows what is expected and how to do everything; and, it takes a much longer time for one person to communicate to 25 others just what to do.

Other teachers of multi-age classrooms report similar occurrences, with their youngest children gaining confidence from trying things they might not have in other situations. The older children encourage the younger ones, and help them stretch and gain confidence. Children who are less academically oriented benefit particularly well, since they might feel intimidated working with an agemate who is more accomplished at a task; yet they do not feel threatened seeking advice or assistance from an older child.

Mixed-age classes have children with an acknowledged variety of background experiences and knowledge. (Of course, unit-aged classes do, too, but we sometimes find ourselves stuck with the concept of "all fourth graders being mostly alike.") Children come to realize that there are differences according to age and to the experiences that they have had. The teacher's responsibility in any classroom is to provide opportunities for all children to learn, to benefit from someone else's different experiences, and to acknowledge the richness of the learning environment when different people contribute in different ways. The child realizes that she is not inferior, just that she has a different background of experiences on a given topic. Avoiding value judgments on differences seems to happen so much more easily in a multi-age classroom. One can readily see, then, that this atmosphere would provide a helpful scaffolding to younger learners. Consequently, they feel comfortable, secure, and normal, rather than overwhelmed and inferior.

Children in unit-graded classrooms are always comparing themselves to or are being compared to children of the same age whether overtly, as in receiving grades, or more subtly among themselves. In these settings there are inherent similar expectations for all children. If a child feels he is not measuring up, it is quite damaging to his attitude about himself as a learner. This can be greatly diminished in a multi-age classroom where the same expectation is not levied on every child.

QUESTION 5: HOW DO YOU ACCOMMODATE THE SUCCESSFUL SOCIAL DEVELOPMENT/PROGRESS OF CHILDREN WHO ARE MIXED IN ONE CLASS?

What could be more natural than functioning in the atmosphere present in family groupings? When the family group is headed by a parent, that parent expects that the older children will be more adept socially, exhibit more mature behaviors, take more responsibility, and continue to grow in all of these areas. The parent, however, also tolerates relapses along the way in this development. The expectations for social development and behavior decrease in proportion to the age of each child. The family group headed by a teacher functions in the same way, with the same tolerances and attitudes toward the social development of the children as a group, and each child as an individual.

The multi-age classroom functions as the family setting, which is the ideal atmosphere in which to mature socially. The multi-age classroom does this naturally, without any manipulation or intervention on the part of the teacher or the administration. The role models are there, present, acting upon the environment. As in any family, of course, all role models are not perfect. When an older child exhibits inappropriate behaviors, whether at home or in the classroom, the situation is dealt with. The teacher values and rewards the appropriate behaviors, and all children learn from this.

With different ages of children, one expects the classroom atmosphere to more naturally accommodate a variety of student needs. When there are a lot of different things going on in the class, the teacher doesn't expect everyone to be doing the same thing. He allows children to have different experiences, provides opportunities for children to work with different and ever-changing groups of children, and ensures that no child is pushed to do something she isn't ready to do. This allows children to do what they are comfortable doing in their social development.

For example, some young students may not be ready to sit still for long periods of time. If the whole class is involved in something that will take an extended period of time, a young child might get up, go quietly to the back of the room, and do something else. Children are at different stages of development, so why require something—such as sitting still—that is so laborious for some? The child who is moving about the room is listening in on things that are of interest to her, and may choose to rejoin the group as her interest is piqued. One can provide for these differences, yet provide opportunities for the child to come back to the group without censure. Although good teachers of unit-graded classes would accommodate individual children in this same way, it seems to happen more naturally in the multi-age class.

Each child in a multi-age situation lives as one of the younger, one of the middle, and one of the older students during his progression through school. Thus, she develops the understanding of and derives from the benefits of each situation. She is challenged, yet supported, when she is a fledgling within the group; as a middle child, she can begin to experience the responsibilities of being a leader while having the older children to go to for advice and assistance; and she can later develop the leadership skills inherent in being one of the oldest. Younger children look up to older children, whether they are the best in the class or not. Just being older in the class knights the child with a prestige she might not enjoy in a class of same-age peers. This progressive, supported maturation is not possible when all children are approximately the same age.

QUESTION 6: WHAT HAPPENS WHEN THESE CHILDREN GO ON TO OTHER, MORE TRADITIONAL CLASSROOMS?

As we have stated throughout, the philosophy of this book presumes holistic teaching with authentic learning experiences, high levels of student inquiry and engagement, student interaction with cooperative and collaborative strategies, quality children's literature, and the other strategies our field has come to associate with implementing a whole language philosophy.

Therefore, the experience we have had with students from multi-age classes returning to or shifting into age-segregated classrooms have more to do with the quality of the individual class than with the style of grouping. For example, if the new classroom to which a student is assigned does not value the self-initiative or independence that has been fostered in the multi-age class, then adjustment can be frustrating.

Adjustments to age-segregated classes have not, in our experience, had anything to do with judgments about their level of knowledge or skills. Academic achievement has not been an issue, at least not one related to their grouping. Where there were children from multi-age classes with learning disabilities, the multi-age class did not cure their disability, but no one would expect it to.

As mentioned in Question 3, we did encounter one case of a gifted child who had been in a multi-age whole language classroom for three years and was eventually promoted to a more traditional, structured fourth grade. This child was intolerably bored in a class where most lessons were teacher centered and instruction was almost entirely whole-group style. This student had been permitted to move at her own pace in her former multi-age class. As a result, she was considerably more advanced than her fourth-grade peers. Had the new fourth grade been more of a whole language setting, there would not have been a problem. But in the structured traditional setting, this little girl was extremely frustrated. After some parent advocacy, the school promoted her to grade five where the content would be more challenging.

Besides academic adjustments, there are social and emotional factors as well. Again, the adjustment of the children into age-segregated classes was more dependent upon the quality of the individual classroom into which the child was placed.

One teacher who inherited several children from the same former multi-age class remarked on the sense of community and caring that they practiced toward each other and its effect on the rest of the classroom. The social skills the children had gained appeared to stay with them into their next grade. Earlier in our study, parents of our multi-age students made unsolicited remarks about how their children were bringing home and practicing their new social skills on their family, especially when there were two or more siblings in the same multi-age class.

To help readers understand the kinds of adjustments required as a child moves from a multi-age classroom to a unit-aged one, we would like to share a story from Dale Woodruff, one of the multi-age teachers from Tallahassee we interviewed for this chapter. Her daughter, Alicia, was among one of the first groups of children to go through their school system in a multi-age model, having been in a grade K–2 (ages 5–8), and a multi-age grade 3–5 (ages 8–11).

When Alicia got to the middle school (grade 6, or 12-year-olds in Florida), she had some adjustments to make after her former supportive environment, but then again, as Dale said, all children entering middle school have adjustments to make. One day, Alicia came home from school upset because all the other kids knew all these "rules" that she said she did not understand. Wisely, Dale comforted her with the fact that she had not spent her life learning these "rules" but could quickly learn them in a few weeks. Alicia's next comment needs no editorial from us. She said, "You know, when I was in elementary school (ages 5–11), it seems as though we learned information and learned about things because we wanted to do it. Now all we do is learn information for the test on Friday."

In closing this chapter, we would like to share the essence of some comments made by our teachers mentioned at the beginning of this chapter. The multi-age classroom provides an opportunity for children to develop cooperative relationships with one another. It addresses and values diversity in people rather than trying to make them into a group with the same knowledge. If children are to be productive, healthy, happy members of society, then working and living with diversity seems to be ideal. The multi-age classroom is really a microcosm of society and provides a unique training ground for life.

REFERENCES

Bizman, A., Yinon, Y., Mivtzari, E., and Shavit, R. (1978). Effects of the age structure of the kindergarten on altruistic behavior. *Journal of School Psychology* 16 (2), 154–160.

—

Buffie, Edward G. (1963). A comparison of mental health and academic achievement: The non graded school vs. the graded school. *Dissertation Abstracts* 23, 4255–A.

—

Carbone, Robert F. (1961). A comparison of graded and non-graded elementary schools. *Elementary School Journal* 62 (2), 82–88.

—

Connell, Donna Reid (1987). The first 30 years were the fairest: Notes from the kindergarten and ungraded primary (K–1–2). *Young Children* 42 (5), 30–68.

—

Day, B., and Hunt, G.H. (1975). Multi-age classrooms: An analysis of verbal communication. *Elementary School Journal* 75 (7), 458–464.

—

Ellison, Alfred (1972). The myth behind graded content. *Elementary School Journal* 72 (4), 212–221.

—

Ford, Bonny E. (1977). Multiage grouping in the elementary school and children's affective development: A review of recent research. *Elementary School Journal* 78 (2), 149–160.

—

Gajadharsingh, J. (1991). The multi-age classroom: Myth and reality. A Canadian study. *The Canadian Education Association Report.*
—

Gilbert, Jerome H. (1962). Multi-graded developmental plan focuses on pupil achievement: Telsa School breaks through traditional graded structure. *Chicago Schools Journal* XLIII (43), 209–214.
—

Gilbert, Jerome H. (1964). Tesla School breaks the lock step. *Elementary School Journal* 64, 306–309.
—

Goldman, J.A. (1981). Social participation of preschool children in same- versus mixed-age groups. *Child Development* 52 (2), 644–650.
—

Goodlad, John I., and Anderson, Robert H. (1987). *The Non-Graded Elementary School,* rev. ed. New York: Teachers College Press.
—

Graziano, W., French, D., and Brownell, C.A., and Hartup, W.W. (1976). Peer interaction in same and mixed age triads in relation to chronological age and incentive condition. *Child Development* 47 (3), 707–714.
—

Halliwell, Joseph W. (1963). A comparison of pupil achievement in graded and non-graded primary classrooms. *Journal of Experimental Education* 32 (1), 59–66.
—

Hamilton, Warren W., and Rehwoldt, Walter (1957). By their differences they learn. *National Elementary Principal* 37, 27–29.
—

Hammack, B.G. (1974). Self-concept: Evaluation of preschool children in single and multi-age classroom settings. Unpublished doctoral dissertation, Texas Women's University. *Dissertation Abstracts International* 35 (10), 6572–6573.
—

Hartup, W.W. (1977). Developmental implication and interactions in same and mixed age situations. *Young Children* 32 (3), 4–13.
—

Hartup, W.W. (1979). The social worlds of childhood. *American Psychologist* 34 (10), 944–950.
—

Hillson, Maurie, Jones, J. Charles, Moore, J. William, and Van Devender, Frank (1965). A Controlled experiment evaluating the effects of a non-graded organization on pupil achievement. In Hillson, Maurie (ed.), *Change and Innovation in Elementary School Organization*. New York: Holt, Rinehart and Winston.

—

Lougee, M.D., Grueneich, R., and Hartup, W.W. (1977). Social interaction in same and mixed-age dyads of preschool children. *Child Development* 48 (3) 1353–1361.

—

MacLachlan, P. (1985). *Sarah Plain and Tall*. New York: Harper & Row, Publishers.

—

Milburn, Dennis (1981). A study of multi-age or family grouped classrooms. *Phi Delta Kappan* 62 (7), 513–514.

—

Moorhouse, E. (1970). The philosophy underlying the British primary school. In Rogers, V.R. (ed.), *Teaching in the British Primary School*. London: The Macmillan Company.

—

Morris. V., Proger, B., and Morrell, J. (1971). Pupil achievement in a nongraded primary plan after 3 and 5 years of instruction. *Educational Leadership* 4 (5), 621–625.

—

Muir, M. (1970). How children take responsibility for their learning. In Rogers, V.R. (ed.), *Teaching in the British Primary School*. London: The Macmillan Company.

—

Piaget, J. (1947). *The Psychology of Intelligence*. London: Routledge & Kegan Paul, Ltd.

—

Pontecorvo, Clotilde, and Zucchermaglio, Cristina (1990). In Goodman, Y.M. (ed.), *How Children Construct Literacy: Piagetian Perspectives*. Newark, DE: International Reading Association, pp. 59–98.

—

Pratt, David. (1986). On the merits of multi-age classrooms. *Research in Rural Education* 3 (3), 111–115.

—

Ridgway, Lorna, and Lawton, Irene (1965). *Family Grouping in the Primary School.* New York: Agathon Press, Inc. and London: Redwood Press, Limited.

—

Schrankler, William J. (1976). Family groupings and the affective domain. *Elementary School Journal* 76 (7), 432–439.

—

Speare, Elizabeth George (1983). *Sign of the Beaver.* New York: Dell Publishing Co., Inc.

—

Stanton, Harry. (1973). Vertical grouping. *Teacher* 90 (5), 106–108.

—

Steere, Bob F. (1972). Non-gradedness: Relevant research for decision making. *Educational Leadership* 29 (8), 709–711.

—

Stehney, Virginia A. (1970). Why multiage grouping in the elementary school? *The National Elementary School Principal* 49 (3), 21–23.

—

Wakefield, A.P. (1979). Multi-age grouping in day care. *Children Today* 8 (3), 26–28.

—

Way, J.W. (1979). Verbal interaction in multi-age classrooms. *Elementary School Journal* 79 (3), 178–186.

—

Wolfson, Bernice J. (1967). The promise of multi-age grouping for individualizing instruction. *Elementary School Journal* 67 (7), 354–363.

—

Zajonc, R.B. and Markus, Gregory B. (1975). Birth order and intellectual development. *Psychological Review* 82 (1), 74–88.

—

RELATED READING

Anderson, Robert H. (1966). Innovations in organization: Theory and practice in the nongraded school. In *Teaching in a World of Change.* New York: Harcourt, Brace, & World, pp. 45-70.

—

Bunting, J.R. (1974). Egocentrism: The effects of social interactions through multi-age grouping. Unpublished doctoral dissertation, State University of New York at Buffalo. *Dissertation Abstracts International* 35 (10), 6356A.

—

Cushman, Kathleen (1990). The whys and hows of the multi-age primary classroom. *American Educator* 14 (2), 28–32 and 39.

—

Di Lorenzo, L.T., and Salter, Ruth (1965). Co-operative research on the nongraded primary. *Elementary School Journal* 65 (5), 269–277.

—

Gartner, Alan, Kohler, Mary C., and Reissman, Frank. (1971). *Children Teach Children: Learning by Teaching.* New York: Harper & Row.

—

Hartup, W.W. (1976). Cross-age versus same-age peer interaction: Ethological and cross-cultural perspectives.In Allen, V.L. (ed.), *Children as Teachers: Theory and Research on Tutoring.* New York: Academic Press, pp. 41–55.

—

McLoughlin, William P. (1970). Continuous pupil progress in the non-graded school: Hope or hoax? *Elementary School Journal* 71 (2), 90–96.

—

McLoughlin, William P. (1969). Evaluation of the non-graded primary. Research Report of the New York State Experimental and Innovative Programs. St. John's University, Jamaica, NY.

—

Muzi, Marialisa (1980). What is meant by school environment: Team teaching and the nongraded school. *Western European Education* 12 (1), 5–37.

—

Oberlander, T.M. (1989). A non-graded multi-age program that works. *Principal* 68 (5), 29–30.

—

Papay, J.P., Costello, R.J., Hedl, J.J., and Speilberger, C.D. (1975). Effects of trait and state anxiety on the performance of elementary school children in traditional and individualized multiage classrooms. *Journal of Educational Psychology* 67 (6), 840–846.

—

Pavan, Barbara Nelson. (1973). Good news: Research on the nongraded elementary school. *Elementary School Journal* 73 (6), 233–242.

—

Pavan, Barbara Nelson (1973). Nongradedness? One view. *Educational Leadership* 30 (5), 401–403.

—

Purdom, Daniel M. (1970). *Exploring the Nongraded School.* Dayton, OH: Institute for Development of Educational Activities, Inc.

—

Rogers, Vincent R. (1970). *Teaching in the British Primary School.* London: The Macmillan Company.

—

Weber, Lillian (1971). The English infant school and informal education. Englewood Cliffs, NJ: Prentice-Hall.

—

INDEX

A

B

C

H

I

J

K

L

M

N

O

P

R

S

T

W

Y

Z

NOTES